Import of the Archive

This book is number five in the Series on Archives, Archivists, and Society, Richard J. Cox, series editor.

Also in the series:

Archival Anxiety and the Vocational Calling, by Richard J. Cox

From Polders to Postmodernism: A History of Archival Theory, by John Ridener

Personal Archives and a New Archival Calling: Readings, Reflections, and Ruminations, by Richard J. Cox

Restoring Order: The Ecole des Chartes and the Organization of Archives and Libraries in France, 1820–1870, by Lara Jennifer Moore

Import of the Archive

U.S. Colonial Rule of the Philippines and the Making of American Archival History

Cheryl Beredo

Litwin Books, LLC
Sacramento, CA

Copyright 2013 Cheryl Beredo

Published by Litwin Books, LLC
PO Box 188784
Sacramento, CA 95818

http://litwinbooks.com/

Layout by Christopher Hagen

This book is printed on acid-free, sustainably-sourced paper.

Library of Congress Cataloging-in-Publication Data

Beredo, Cheryl.
 Import of the archive : U.S. colonial rule of the Philippines and the making of American archival history / Cheryl Beredo.
   pages cm. -- (Series on archives, archivists and society ; number. 5)
 Includes bibliographical references and index.
  Summary: "Examines the role of archives in the United States' colonization of the Philippines between 1898 and 1916"--Provided by publisher.
 ISBN 978-1-936117-72-7 (alk. paper)
 1. Archives--Philippines--History. 2. Archives--United States--History. 3. United States. Philippine Commission (1900-1916) 4. Philippines--History--1898-1946. I. Philippines. Bureau of Archives II. Title.
 CD2213.B47 2013
 025.3'414--dc23
                              2013006911

Table of Contents

Acknowledgments .... *vii*

Introduction 1
Archives And War 15
Archives And Anti-Imperialism 43
Archives And Land 63
Conclusion 89

Endnotes *105*
Bibliography *137*
Index *151*

ACKNOWLEDGMENTS

Many people and institutions have helped to make this book happen, and I owe a debt of gratitude to all of them.

Several institutions supported the dissertation research that made the writing of this book possible. The East-West Center, Smithsonian Institution, Massachusetts Historical Society, and Bentley Historical Library provided fellowships that allowed me the time and other resources to conduct the research for this book. Grants from the University of Hawai'i at Mānoa supported my travel to archives and libraries in College Park and Manila. The archivists and librarians at the National Archives, National Anthropological Archives, Smithsonian Institution Archives, Massachusetts Historical Society, Bentley Historical Library, Special Collections at the University of Michigan, Philippine National Library, American Historical Collections at Ateneo de Manila, and the Division of Rare and Manuscript Collections at Cornell University made doing this research a special treat.

Professors at Cornell University, the University of Pittsburgh, and the University of Hawai'i at Mānoa have taught me much over the years and guided me along the way. Jacqueline Goldsby helped me to learn the joys of archival research. Elizabeth DeLoughrey encouraged me to think about the Philippines in the context of the Pacific and gave me the nudge to move to Hawai'i. Richard Cox taught me to think like an archivist. At the University of Hawai'i at Mānoa, I owe thanks to the faculty of the Department of American Studies, Ruth Mabanglo, Haunani-Kay Trask, and Katerina Teaiwa. I owe special thanks to my dissertation committee: Vernadette Gonzalez, Karen Kosasa, Vina Lanzona, Robert Perkinson, and Mari Yoshihara.

Friends and family have been my greatest pleasure, and they have helped me through this process in many ways. Special thanks to K-Sue Park, Matt Tierney, Kate Rubin, Susannah Mira, and Anthony Reed for their friendship. Liz Muller has been so wonderfully, unbelievably supportive through this process. I dedicate this book to my family—Elisa, Pedro, and Chris—whose patience and goodwill have made all the difference. A heartfelt thanks to all.

CHAPTER 1
INTRODUCTION

Between 1898 and 1916, the United States ruled the Philippines with true gusto. Having successfully suppressed the Philippine Revolution and started the American occupation of the islands, the United States was poised to establish its influence far beyond its continental borders. The United States Philippine Commission, composed of Americans and headed by William Howard Taft, worked in earnest to establish a robust colonial government that would exploit the islands' natural resources and expand its modest economy. To this end, the commission passed dozens of laws within weeks of assuming authority in the islands, concerning itself with the construction of roads and bridges, improvement to ports and harbors, establishment of universal education, and promotion of sanitary and public health initiatives. In the first two decades of the United States' occupation of the Philippines, Americans made their presence definitively known.

It would have been impossible, for example, to live in Manila and not notice the United States forces hunkered down in the city's various administrative buildings, which had formerly housed the Spanish colonial regime. The arrival of schoolteachers from the United States was heralded in the media with great enthusiasm. In short, some aspects of the United States colonial rule were incessantly touted, evidence of Americans dutifully bearing, in the parlance of Rudyard Kipling, the "White Man's Burden." American administrators bemoaned Filipinos' "misunderstanding" of the United States' good intentions in the Philippines.

At first blush, this episode in American political history seems unrelated to American archival history. The United States' activities in Asia appear to have little to do with the establishment of archives at home, and it has become a truism in American archival history that archival principles in the United States were adapted from those established in Europe. However, this book suggests that, upon closer examination, American empire-building and archive-building are not unrelated historical phenomenon. Rather, each was critical to the other, helping to create a cultural logic that made both important for that historic moment. By thinking of archival history within the frame of colonial history, archivists can better understand our roles in the societies that we document and more critically evaluate the historical record that we steward.

***

On the eve of the twentieth century, the United States ruled over more people and land than ever before. The influx of European immigrants, the phenomenal growth of cities, and the country's expanding industrial economy changed American life. As for land, through wars of conquest, land treaties, and purchase–namely, the Louisiana Purchase (1803), Adams-Onis Treaty (1819), Texas annexation (1845), Oregon Treaty (1846), Mexican cession (1848), Gadsden Purchase (1853), and the Alaska Purchase (1867)—the continental United States had grown significantly in the nineteenth century. For some, overseas expansion was antithetical to the country's republican tradition and detrimental to American life. Such American luminaries as Mark Twain, Andrew Carnegie, and Samuel Gompers weighed in on this issue, publicly, cogently, and repeatedly arguing against establishing sovereignty in faraway lands.

For others, the United States' constant growth and expansion in the nineteenth century was itself significant and formative. It prompted historian Frederick Jackson Turner to go so far as to posit that America's national identity was actually defined by the country's relationship to the western frontier. In his influential 1893 essay, "The Significance of the Frontier in American History," he argued, "Up to our own day American history has been in a large degree the history of the colonization of the Great West. The existence of an area of free land, its continuous recession, and the advance of American settlement westward, explain American development."[1] Thus at the end of the nineteenth century, questions that emerged were: More? And if so, where next?

At roughly the same moment that the United States was pondering these questions, the Philippines, which had been under Spanish colonial rule for roughly three hundred years, was also poised for change. The Spanish state had been both evangelistic and despotic, establishing churches throughout the islands but also ruling with a harshness that earned the islanders' animosity. In 1887, Jose Rizal depicted the harshness of Spanish rule in *Noli Me Tangere*, the first of two novels that skewered the colonial state, and for his critique, the state rewarded him first with exile and ultimately with execution. In 1896, Rizal's death, decades of sporadic peasant uprisings, and growing discontent among the society's elites erupted into the Philippine Revolution.

In 1898, when the U.S.S. Maine exploded off the shores of Cuba and the United States suspected that Spain was responsible, the United States involved itself in the revolution to oust the Spanish colonial state in Cuba. With these developments, the people of the Philippines seemed to have found an ally in ending the old empire in their part of the world as well. To further weaken Spain, the United States dispatched naval ships to Manila Bay—practically on the other side of the world—to defeat the colonial forces there. This conflict involving Spain, the United States, Cuba, and the Philippines came to be known as the Spanish-American War, and was dubbed a "splendid little war" because it was a short conflict from which the United States emerged victorious without question.

The dominant narrative at the time was simple and heroic. Since 1895 the United States had observed the uprising in Cuba against Spain. With the destruction of the U.S.S. Maine in 1898, the United States was compelled to go to war that year. The jingoist press, most notably personified by newspaper magnate William Randolph Hearst, covered the war extensively, sending correspondents to report back to an American readership hungry for military glory. Such stories complemented the notion that just as the United States was fighting alongside Cuban revolutionaries, so too would the United States come to the aid of freedom fighters in the Philippines. For Americans at that end of the nineteenth century, such an understanding of the country's noble motivations legitimated the United States' involvement in areas beyond its national, continental borders.

The Treaty of Paris was signed in 1898 and ratified in 1899, ending the Spanish-American War, a splendid little war or not. Though it officially ended hostilities between Spain and the United States, it spelled trouble for United States-Philippine relations. The prize sought after years of struggle—sovereignty over the islands—was not awarded to Filipino revolutionaries, but to the United States per a clause in the Treaty of Paris that transferred the Philippines, Puerto Rico, and Guam for a sum of twenty million dollars. When the United States acquired these islands and parts of Cuba per the agreement, the story of American altruism would be lost without some cultural logic that made the country's new imperial role palatable. In the Philippines, this was articulated through the "Benevolent Assimilation" proclamation. Issued by President McKinley shortly after the United States' arrival in the islands, this policy noted that

> It should be the earnest wish and paramount aim of the military administration to win the confidence, respect, and affection of the inhabitants of the Philippines by assuring them in every possible way that full measure of individual rights and liberties which is the heritage of free peoples, and by proving to them that the mission of the United States is one of benevolent assimilation substituting the mild sway of justice and right for arbitrary rule.[2]

Thus intended to assure the islands' population of the good will and good intentions of the new occupation forces, the proclamation was the way to recuperate the image of national virtue by suggesting that American colonialism was better than European colonialism.

The "Benevolent Assimilation" proclamation did not assuage the revolutionary forces, as within months of its issuance, the United States and the Philippines were at war. Known as the Philippine-American War (1898-1902), this conflict was characterized by ambitiously atrocious acts, such as burning of villages, "reconcentrating" residents into makeshift camps, and torturing persons of interest. The American military's other violent excesses were later the subject of federal and public scrutiny, but by then, the damage to the archipelago's population and United States-Philippine relations was done. Thus, when United States declared victory of the Philippine-American War in 1902 and began the work of civil colonial government in earnest, it was with cruel irony that the island's population might recall United States President William McKinley's "Benevolent Assimilation" proclamation of December 1898, an announcement of Americans' goodwill toward Filipinos.

It was in this political context that the American colonial state established and developed a robust archives program in the islands. While informed by the political vagaries associated with establishing a new colonial regime in a war-torn land, those conditions did not prevent the Philippine Commission from devoting energy and resources to the development of the Bureau of Archives. The bulk of the archives came from the outgoing Spanish colonial government, but as the new government became more entrenched, the archives grew accordingly.

Despite never generating public excitement as did the establishment of universal education or the construction of inland roads, the state's archival collections proved highly valuable to the state's projects. Changes in the scope and administration of the archives, for example, ensured that the institution did not merely reflect the work of the new colonial state, but aided in it. The archives provided information needed to begin new projects or improve upon projects undertaken under the Spanish regime, and served as an active participant in the entrenchment and operation of new institutions under the American regime. Indeed, the following chapters will show that the obscure but certainly ambitious work of the Bureau of Archives was critical to the colonial state's realization of its more spectacular work in the Philippines.

To begin to understand how this could have been the case, it is helpful to parse the establishment and growth of the colonial state's archives into phases: Archives of the Crown of Spain (1898-1901), Bureau of Archives in the Department of Public Instruction (1901-1905), Division of Archives, Patents, Copyrights and Trademarks in the Executive Bureau (1905-1916), and the Division of Archives, Patents, Trademarks, and Copyrights of the Philippine Library and Museum in the Department of Public Instruction (1916).

The most obvious and dramatic transition was in 1899, when Spain transferred its archives relating to colonial administration to the United States. Changes thereafter within the United States colonial government were reflected in significant changes in the purpose and orientation of the archives. Established in 1901 as part of the Department of Public Instruction, the unit charged primarily with the establishment of universal public education in the islands, the archives were moved to the Executive Bureau for more than a decade. During its time in the Executive Bureau from 1905 to 1916, the archives' role expanded to include not just inactive records, but also "live" records directly related to the growth of industry in the islands, e.g., patents, trademarks, and copyrights. With the passage of the Jones Act in 1916, which outlined the Philippines' long road to sovereignty, the archives were returned to the Department of Public Instruction, but this time within the largest government-supported cultural institution in the islands at that time, the Philippine Library and Museum. Thus the archives took the form that is familiar to archivists and historians today—a Philippine cultural institution oriented to the public, focused on the history of the islands and its people.

How did this often-overlooked aspect of the American presence in the islands function before it became that well-known research and educational institution? Why should archivists care?

Exploring the answers to this question, *Import of the Archive* first subverts the notion that archives simply reflect or document the society of which they are a part, then suggests that indeed archives help in the making of that society. While this seems a modest assertion, such an evaluation by archivists is timely considering how the United States' colonial rule of the Philippines has been viewed in recent historical scholarship. Historians from a range of fields and approaches—including scholars of the Philippines, United States, cultural and military historians, and even scholars in the history of science—have re-evaluated the question of American benevolence, considering how notions of race and science at the time, for example, affected the outcomes and meanings of United States-Philippine relations.

In April 1898, the United States offered military aid in the Filipinos' war against the Spanish colonial state, along with the assurance that the United States had little interest in maintaining control of the islands after the conflict was resolved.[3] However, after Admiral Dewey's victory at Manila Bay and the ratification of the Treaty of Paris, it became clear that such unofficial assurances would not be honored. While the exact nature of the negotiations between the United States and the Philippines and the United States and Spain before the start of the Philippine-American War remains uncertain, scholars agree that the violence during the official course of the war (1899-1902) and in subsequent years is indisputable.

In the United States, the most spectacular aspect of that violence at the time was the Americans' "water cure" torture of native combatants and massacre of native civilians. Military historian David Silbey observes that, while the water cure was not more prevalent than other forms of torture, its brutality "captured the imagination of observers and historians alike."[4] The United States retaliation after the "Balangiga Massacre" by indiscriminate, summary execution of villagers on Samar, likewise caught the attention of the United States media.[5] Indeed, the legacies of the United States military's misconduct in the Philippines continue to attract a popular readership today.[6]

Racial ideology accounts, at least in part, for the brutality of the United States forces in the Philippines. Depictions of natives as children, or likening Filipinos to Native and African Americans, worked to legitimate the United States' war in the islands.[7] At the same time, such depictions served to re-assert the racial identity, namely the whiteness, of Americans; and though such differentiation would raise questions about how the United States might reasonably expect to "uplift" the natives so different from themselves, the dynamic between the mutually constitutive categories of "white Americans" and "brown Filipinos" would later well serve the colonial state.[8]

The conflict was a complicated and ambitious affair that demanded the mobilization of resources and extensive disciplinary measures. That is, in addition to the brute force of military conflict, a United States victory over the Philippines required "intimate and continuous surveillance" through reconcentration policies of 1901 and 1902, responses to the cholera epidemic of 1902 and 1903, and the census from 1903-1905.[9] The creation of "protected zones," wherein villagers would be placed after their homes and villages were burned, Philippine social historian Reynaldo Ileto argues, were not only cruel; they served to establish boundaries that, in turn, prevented "the movement of people in and out, enabling their surveillance, and inducing them to want and to do what the occupation army wanted."[10] The United States' occupying force's response to cholera epidemic of 1902 and 1903 strongly resembled the force's reconcentration policy. Warwick Anderson, an historian of science, observes that "The Philippine health service remained, above all, an organization on the march: when cholera broke out, military administrative logic suggested it seek intelligence, send out sanitary squads, burn houses, and isolate troublemakers, in the same way the army had suppressed or diverted *insurrectos* in the archipelago."[11] In the case of the census from 1903 to 1905, as Philippine historian Vicente Rafael demonstrates, census-takers and those individuals they questioned were subject to surveillance; the former by their supervisors and the latter by the census-takers.[12] As crucially, the structure of the census offered the tools for "imagining the terms of colonial society as, above all, a racial hierarchy."[13]

In this context, the Bureau of Archives helped to create a narrative in which the United States was a benevolent colonial ruler. For a time, for example, the colonial government sought to establish a culture of homesteading in the Philippines modeled on what had transpired in nineteenth century America, with the idea of spreading the populace throughout the archipelago and encouraging the growth of agriculture. During this period, the Bureau of Archives served as the registrar of active land patents and thus was responsible, while working in collaboration with the Bureau of Lands, for the proper filing and approval of requests for homesteads. In this instance, the Bureau of Archives was not simply the place that preserved the land patents, it was the bureau that helped to register new patents. Thus, the archives was one in a constellation of colonial government bureaus that shifted the way land tenure was structured, and the United States promoted this as a positive and progressive change.

The colonial state's archive also helped to create the related narrative that the primary characteristic of United States-Philippine relations was tutelary. Describing the period of United States rule, Philippine historian Ruby R. Paredes's used the term, "the paradox of Philippine colonial democracy."[14] This paradox is perhaps best illustrated by consideration of the United States' establishment of a colonial government, its varying regional policies, and the racial logic that underlay both. Such consideration also suggests the validity of anthropologist Nicholas Thomas's argument that the power of the colonial state is never monolithic or complete.[15]

The United States touted its colonization of the Philippines as an exceptional project that differed from European colonization of other parts of the world insofar as it sought to establish modern institutions of government, including public education and popularly elected officials.[16] As Romeo V. Cruz has demonstrated, however, in at least one operational and bureaucratic aspect, the United States handling of its overseas territories was very much modeled on European institutions. Despite never having been named explicitly so, the Bureau of Insular Affairs, in its various permutations between 1898 and 1934, served as the United States' colonial office on par with similar institutions of European countries. Cruz notes: "The BIA was one of the administrative and institutional consequences of America's response to imperialism, an agency as equally effective (at least in theory) as that organized by Spain or by other colonial European powers."[17]

While the question of whether the United States has been exceptional in its dealings with its colonies was, and continues to be, debated, the enthusiasm with which the United States promoted its colonial agenda was undeniable. This enthusiasm was not only due to the conditions that American military and colonial officials found in the islands; as Warwick Anderson and political scientist Patricio Abinales have respectively argued, the Philippines served as a laboratory for the newest available tropical science and as a battleground for Progressive and Machine politicians in the United States.[18] Historian Glenn Anthony May addresses both of these points, by way of providing an account of the policies of the colonial state during the Taft era (1900-1913) that disputes the success of the United States' colonial state in the Philippines. He argues that American policy-makers, especially the Philippine Commission, used American models of "New England town government" and "the educational theories of Thomas Jefferson" to formulate three types of colonial policy: "preparing Filipinos to exercise governmental responsibilities; providing primary education for the masses; and developing the economy."[19] He concludes that the Taft Era was more a "brief "deviation"" in Philippine history, rather than its formative period; he notes "On the balance, the Philippines remained fundamentally Filipino there was far more continuity than change."[20] The notion was that in European colonialism, the metropole exploited its colonies for maximum material gain, the United States was involved in a kind of experiment whereby the primary purpose of colonial rule was to prepare Filipinos for self-governance.

Indeed, debate over whether the United States ought to be involved in the Philippines at all often pivoted on this question. Was the United States going to exploit the resources of the islands? If so, would Americans or Filipinos stand to gain? Would American really be able to teach Filipinos to govern themselves? If so, how long would it take? If not, would the United States maintain control of the Philippines indefinitely?

The most dramatic example of this in the context of the Bureau of Archives relates to the bureau's administration. Given that the Philippines was not to become a colony settled by Americans, the United States' creation and maintenance of a colonial government required the participation and cooperation of the native population. As Norman G. Owen has noted, "By 1899, the United States was already looking for Filipino leaders with whom a *modus vivendi* could be arranged, a means of saving not only the costs of representation and local administration, but also what was left of her ideals and self-image."[21] The American policy of so-called Filipinization, from the Taft era through the Francis Burton Harrison administration, worked to centralize the colonial government.[22] Filipinization allowed that whenever Filipinos proved to be capable to hold positions within the civil service, they should be thus appointed, and after the arrival of new Governor-General Francis Burton Harrison in 1913, this policy appeared to be more aggressively implemented.

One controversial element of Filipinization was the question of what this would mean for Americans in the colonial government. In 1916, with the creation of the Philippine Library and Museum and the appointment of Teodoro Kalaw as director, units within the new organization that had historically been headed by Spaniards and Americans would report to a Filipino for the first time in history. Manuel Yriarte was the head of the Bureau of Archives under the Spanish government, continued on in that role upon the transition to an American government, and stayed on longer still as Filipinos came to hold appointed and elected office. However, Director of the Philippine Library James Robertson, an American who had built his career on the history of the Philippines under Spanish rule, elected to resign from his post and return to the United States. In this instance, while Yriarte's continuing appointment suggests a level of stability, the Bureau of Archives was in the middle of this question of the meaning and consequences of American tutelage of Filipinos.

Thus, the archives were part of the politics of the colonial state, not simply the documentarian of the United States' benevolence and tutelage. Appreciating the role of the archives in the construction of narratives of American progressivism is not only useful for gaining a more complex appreciation of the Bureau of Archives' institutional history; it is also critical for understanding how the bureau helped to make the United States, and its imperial adventures, worth documenting.

In considering how the archives made the American project in the Philippines worth documenting, this study sheds light on the archives' self-perpetuating logical value. It argues that the archive was important insofar as it served the political needs of the moment: it made the case for the "benevolence" of American occupation, by holding the voluminous records of a modern bureaucracy. The archive provided a narrative of progress, by merging its work with the libraries and museums of the islands. In other words, it offered *the foundation for the more spectacular colonial projects*—building roads and schools, opening the government service to Filipinos, holding open elections—that the United States touted as the differences between American and European colonialism.

An essential element of the foundation for these more spectacular projects was the conditions of a peaceful, colonial civil society. And in this area, too, the archives served a purpose. They helped to obscure the messy violence of American rule by their precise and scientific constitutional form. Compared alongside the war that raged on between United States and Philippine forces, all of the proposed and enacted administrative changes to the Bureau of Archives were clean, simple, and logical, even when the execution of those changes was not. It provided the administrative structure, mapped the official channels of communication, and supplied historical information needed for the American colonial state's improvement upon the preceding, Spanish regime.

By thus serving as an active institution in the execution of civil colonial projects, demonstrating the benevolence of American rule, and obscuring its unsavory aspects, the archives offered, perhaps most importantly, *flexibility*. Examined closely and in context, single institutions can help to provide more complex understandings about a larger political culture or phenomena. In other words, how this small bureau in the colonial government was conceptualized, established, developed and, at times, undermined, can serve as a window onto other matters facing United States colonialism in the islands. In light of the institutional changes it underwent between 1898 and 1916, the colonial archive could support the political needs of the administration at any moment. Sometimes these had to do with familiarizing the administration with the landscape of war, the disposition and naming of public lands, the registry of private property, or the development of a model labor force. With its rich and complex history, the archive is a most important and enduring technology of colonial rule.

Covering the period between 1898 and 1916, this book's chronological scope includes both Republican and Democratic Presidents of the United States and Republican and Democratic Governor-Generals of the Philippines, thus encompassing three major periods of the United States colonial period in the Philippines. From 1898 to 1902, the Philippine Revolution, Spanish-American War, and Philippine-American War were being fought. Between 1901 and 1913, the imprint of William Howard Taft on the colonial policy in the islands would be difficult to ignore and from 1913 to 1916, Francis Burton Harrison's administration left its own mark by aggressively pursuing and implementing the policy of Filipinization.

Between 1901 and 1913, William Howard Taft played varied, but always important, roles in the government of the islands. In 1900, he served as the head of the second United States Philippine Commission, also known as the Taft Commission. From 1901 to 1903, Taft was the Governor-General of the Philippines. Though Taft left his post as Governor-General to return to the United States in 1904, he did so to become Secretary of War in President Theodore Roosevelt's administration. Holding that position until 1908, Taft was the highest-ranking United States official to whom the colonial government reported, before reaching President Roosevelt. The Governor-General reported to the Chief of Bureau of Insular Affairs who reported to Secretary of War Taft. Of course, as President of the United States from 1909 to 1913, Taft was the absolute highest-ranking official in the United States and contended to maintain an interest in the Philippines. Taft's ascension to the United States presidency by way of the Philippines and avowed continued interest and affection for the islands, perhaps predictably, led to the naming of the "Taft Era."

During the period between 1913 and 1921, when Francis Burton Harrison served as Governor-General, the new administration's policy was alternately viewed as a period of sharp divergence from the policies during the "Taft Era" or a more aggressive continuance of its policies. Prior to his appointment to the highest office in the Philippine government, Harrison had served in the United States House of Representatives, a Democrat from New York with well-known anti-imperialist sentiments. Some viewed his appointment as a cynical political move to rid the United States of a party deadweight. Others considered his appointment as a clear indicator, given Harrison's anti-imperialist views, of President Woodrow Wilson's intentions in the Philippines. In any event, every aspect of Harrison's administration was overshadowed by the controversy surrounding Filipinization, or the appointment of Filipinos to positions in the government service, and represented the starkest difference between the rules of Taft and Harrison. Given this purported difference, this book treats, to a degree, the political issues that defined the praise and condemnation of both Republican and Democratic rule.

By focusing on the Bureau of Archives throughout these years, we can trace the continuities between the two parties' policies in the islands. This is possible for two reasons. First, the colonial government's archives were understood by all of the Governor-Generals to be of use to the business of governing the islands, resulting in a steady amount of attention being paid to archives and recordkeeping systems throughout the period and, in turn, legislation and other government documents to analyze.

The second reason, related to the first, is that the colonial archives and the recordkeeping systems that channeled government documents into the archives tended not to be the showcase of any administration. If an administration wanted to demonstrate its order and efficiency, it might highlight the improved operations of the Customs House; if the administration wanted to highlight industry and economy of energy, it might highlight the construction of roads and bridges. By contrast, because the Bureau of Archives was not an exemplar of American ingenuity and efficiency, it garnered very little media coverage. The Bureau of Archives' cross-referencing systems and filing cabinets were the unremarkable workhorses of the bureaucracy, only drawing the attention of the colonial administration when they faltered.

Thus, this book supposes that any existing documentation on the Bureau of Archives had little currency beyond the administrators who either produced the records or whom received them. Because these records were unlikely to be of interest to anyone not directly related to them, they lacked the partisan language that often accompanied any administration's description of other aspects of United States rule. As the later chapters will show, however, the absence of partisan language does not necessarily mean the absence of political meaning.

In addition to a clearly delineated chronological scope, the following chapters also have a delineated topical scope. This study of the archive of the United States' colonial government in the Philippines draws almost exclusively on the sources generated by that government and on sources created by individuals who, though not officially tied with the colonial government, were very closely associated to it. The following pages will take the "archive" to mean (a) government documents, published or unpublished, of the Spanish regime that were ceded by Spain to the United States to form the core of the Bureau of Archives or its later iterations (b) government documents, published or unpublished, of the American regime that were transferred to the Bureau of Archives (or its later iterations) and (c) historical manuscripts acquired by the American colonial government—by seizure, purchase, or reproduction in the United States, Philippines or Spain—to enrich the collections of the Bureau of Archives or its later iterations. Documentation in the United States that expressly contradicted the archives described above will also be considered, especially as such records formed a kind of unofficial archive that presented an alternative record on the United States' involvement in the Philippines.

This book focuses on the United States' activities in the Philippines, and the sources upon which it relies are those created by Americans about the Philippines for, generally, consumption by Americans either in the colonial government in the Philippines or the United States government in Washington, D.C. This book does not include analysis of the records of the Philippine Revolutionary Government except insofar as they appear in what the United States Department of War called the Philippine Insurgent Records. Examination of anti-colonial perspectives is limited to those Americans generally associated with the activities of the Anti-Imperialist League, an organization with very close ties to representatives in the United States government. The myriad speeches, fiction, and drama of the period—both in the United States and the Philippines—are not analyzed per se in this book. When they do appear, they do so in the context of specific authors' and other agitators' interactions with the colonial government, usually as a result of the Sedition Law, Flag Law, or other censorship measure. Put simply, this book focuses on the records created by the colonial government for the colonial government; outsiders—Filipinos, American civilians, and other foreigners in the islands—make appearances only insofar as they transact business of one kind or another with the colonial government.

While such an understanding of "colonial archive" may seem rather narrow, the body of material encompassed by this definition is actually quite voluminous. Indeed, in analyzing the material that the colonial government itself defined as its archive, this book follows Ann Laura Stoler's suggestion to read "along the archival grain"—to attempt to understand the colonial project as simultaneously powerful and fragile, as at once repressive and unsure, as both ideally ordered and manifestly unruly.[23] In the context of the United States' rule of the Philippines, colonial projects were all of these things, as well as ambitious and tutelary: roads were supposed to bring economic development; schools were supposed to mold model citizens; civil service regulations were supposed to yield skilled laborers, and a bicameral legislature was supposed to transform Filipinos into self-governable subjects. The archives both documented and helped to realize these projects of the colonial government.

This book supposes that such an approach to reading, often reserved for analyzing the absences in a conventional historical record, may be fruitfully applied to those conventional historical records themselves. Accepting the argument that some records, such as those of the colonial archive, as delineated here, obscure other and dissenting perspectives, this book then goes on to ask: *how* do these official records function to obscure? What was the organizational structure that enabled such elision? To what effect?

By examining how the colonial archive's different iterations facilitated the entrenchment and normalization of the United States colonial administration of the Philippines, we can see what made the institution so effective. Indeed, while the history of the Bureau of Archives has been so readily overlooked, this book begins from the premise that there are political meanings and material consequences in the archiving of everyday communications. Moreover, while the archives was presumed to render special the records held therein, the following chapters will demonstrate that the more significant achievement of the colonial archive was otherwise: it transformed records of remarkable events—imperial conquest and colonial governance—into matters of routine business.

CHAPTER 2
ARCHIVES AND WAR

"No war ever left such a wonderful mass of material for historians."
--Henry Watterson, *History of the Spanish-American War*[24]

Introduction

Though considered minor military conflicts today and "splendid" to some in their time, the Spanish-American War (1898) and the Philippine-American War (1899-1902) were significant, devastating wars for the people of the Philippines who sought independence from colonial rule. The Spanish-American War was an interruption of the Philippine Revolution, when the United States became involved in the Philippine Republic's cause to overthrow Spanish rule in the islands. The Philippine-American War was a continuation of the Philippine Revolution, this time with the Philippine Republic fighting the establishment of American rule in the islands. These conflicts were tremendously generative of archival material about the Philippines for the United States. These materials were used to articulate the case for United States sovereignty as well as the argument for Philippine independence.

The United States acquired Spain's colonial archives of the Philippines per the Treaty of Paris in 1898, but in the years after the Treaty of Paris as the Philippine-American War raged on, archives in the islands ceased to be only a matter of post-Spanish-American War spoils. As Henry Watterson suggests, there existed an awareness of the moment's historic importance and attention to the archives that would help make sense of it. Of course, the "yellow journalism" of the period provided voluminous, if not always reliable, accounts of events in the Spanish-American War theaters. Meanwhile, United States officials predictably spent a considerable amount of time creating a record of comparable scale, accounting for why the nation's involvement in the Philippines was justified. A variety of groups had a stake, whether economic or political, in their account of the United States' involvement gaining widespread credibility.

This chapter explores the ways in which archives figured into how the United States waged its war in the islands. It begins with a closer examination of the Treaty of Paris as it related to archives and considers a question of access nearly a decade later, shedding light on the changing uses of the archives. This chapter also reviews the work of Captain John R.M. Taylor on the papers that came to be known as the Philippine Insurgent Papers, or the Philippine Revolutionary Papers, and the controversy surrounding their compilation and deferred publication. Finally, this chapter analyzes a selection of the translated documents of the Philippine government that were created at the height of its hostilities with Spain and the United States and outlined principles and procedures for archives under independent Philippine rule. Taken together, these "flashpoints" in the relationship between archives and war show that while the archive is most generally and readily understood as an entity of civil rule, as evidenced by the Philippine Commission's many acts related thereto, the archive has undeniable martial origins and, thus, martial legacies.

Treaty of Paris and the Spanish Colonial Government's Archive

On December 10, 1898, representatives of the United States and Spain signed the Treaty of Paris to end the Spanish-American War. In addition to ending hostilities between the two countries, the treaty also provided for the United States' purchase of the Philippines, Guam, and Puerto Rico. An infrequently-cited section of the treaty addressed the United States taking possession of more than Spain's colonial territories; section eight of the Treaty of Paris provided for the cession of Spanish archives relating to the Philippines to the United States. Per this section, "all the buildings, wharves, barracks, forts, structures, public highways and other immovable property which, in conformity with law, belong to the public domain" of the Philippines were ceded to the United States, as well as the documentation related thereto:

> The aforesaid relinquishment or cession, as the case may be, includes all documents exclusively referring to the sovereignty relinquished or ceded that may exist in the archives of the Peninsula. Where any document in such archives only in part relates to said sovereignty, a copy of such part will be furnished whenever it shall be requested. Like rules shall be reciprocally observed in favor of Spain in respect of documents in the archives of the islands above referred to.
> In the aforesaid relinquishment or cession, as the case may be, are also included such rights as the Crown of Spain and its authorities possess in respect of the official archives and records, executive as well as judicial, in the islands above referred to, which relate to said islands or the rights and property of their inhabitants. Such archives and records shall be carefully preserved, and private persons shall without distinction have the right to require, in accordance with law, authenticated copies of the contracts, wills and other instruments forming part of notorial protocols or files, or which may be contained in the executive or

judicial archives, be the latter in Spain or in the islands aforesaid.²⁵

In other words, Spain ceded documents that in their entirety related to the administration of the United States' newly acquired territory. In instances where documents only partly related to that administration, Spain was obliged to provide a reproduction of the document upon request. Per the peace treaty, in addition to claiming ownership of "official archives and records," the United States was obliged to care for them as well, to see that such archives and records, especially executive and judicial records, were "carefully preserved." Further, the United States was obliged to make accessible "without distinction" to private persons "authenticated copies of contracts, wills and other instruments forming part of notorial protocols or files, or which may be contained in the executive or judicial archives." In short, the Treaty of Paris provided the new American regime with the core archival records needed to administer the old Spanish colony and, in so doing, gave that nascent archive's custodians a hint of the shape of things to come.

In addition to acquiring the Spanish records relating to immovable property on land annexed by the United States per the Treaty of Paris, the United States acquired records relating to the land itself in the public domain, or public lands. The mandate for the care for this series of records was embodied in Philippine Commission Act No. 218 (September 2, 1901), "An Act Creating a Bureau of Public Lands." Per this act, the first of the appointed chief of the bureau's duties was "to collect and safely keep all existing Spanish records relating to the public lands or their conveyances." The collection and safekeeping of these Spanish records, scattered throughout the archipelago in provincial offices, was important for determining the extent of public lands upon annexation and the disposition of public lands as the colonial state entrenched itself.

According to Manuel Yriarte, "the keeper of archives" under the Spanish regime and the first Chief of the Bureau of Archives under the American regime, the treaty was effectively observed. Records transferred after the change in colonial administration, included "all subjects connected with the Spanish Administration and all institutions affected by Spanish legislation."²⁶ Yriarte described a veritable trove of information about the previous colonial administration:

> It embraces papers relating to the general administration of the Archipelago, the municipalities, civil and religious corporations, colleges, hospitals, pious foundations, banks and mercantile corporations, consulates, printing offices, colonies, penal institutions, Chinese immigration, patents and trademarks, personal records of officials, public charity and health, public instruction, post and telegraph, market license contracts, cock-pits, weights and measures, ferries,

opium, construction and repair of State, Provincial and Municipal buildings, bridges, wagon roads, railroads and tramways, industrial, urban, cedula and Chinese head taxes, custom duties, revenue from stamped paper, revenue from *vino* and tobacco when these articles were monopolies of the States, sale of State lands, security fund, and various other matters.[27]

And this was just a partial description of the archives transferred to the United States' government in the Philippines per the Treaty of Paris.

In addition to accepting this mass of records ceded by Spain, the Philippine Commission worked to actively gather information about archives in the islands. The Philippine Commission passed a resolution on May 6, 1901, requesting that the Military Governor of the islands require from District Commanders reports on public records in the districts throughout the archipelago. These reports were to include, "descriptions of the several classes of papers preserved, the period covered by them, their state as to preservation and completeness, and such other information as may contribute to a complete understanding of the condition of the public records of the Philippine Islands."[28] While the scope of this reporting system was ambitious, its findings were discouraging: some records were destroyed during battle; others were destroyed either by officers of the Spanish Government or the Revolutionary Government.[29] Nevertheless, the Philippine Commission resolution, the Military Governor's general orders, and District Commanders' reports all illustrate the United States' mindfulness of the importance of Spanish archives to the United States' presence in the Philippines between the years 1898 and 1901.

These were the conditions of the transfer of archives from Spain to the United States and the archives' subsequent growth through the U.S. military's findings throughout the islands. They began as awards for winning the Spanish-American War, and as this chapter will show, became useful for waging the Philippine-American War. Before launching into an examination of the archives and war, it is useful to pause and consider the change in the usage and primary purpose of these archives over the course of the United States' colonial rule of the Philippines. This is evident in a question about access to them roughly a decade after their transfer. Writing to the Philippine Commission's Executive Secretary in 1912, Philippine Library Director James Alexander Robertson noted that

> The librarian believes that the leniency should not extend to the voluntary relinquishment of a body of documents that are so valuable for the history of the Philippine Islands, and which are in great part mere dead material in the Archives of Spain. The history of the Philippine Islands is daily assuming large propor-

tions among the Filipinos, and these documents will have a great use here.[30]

Robertson described the United States' assertion of claims on Spanish archives permitted by the 1898 Treaty of Paris as minimal, and the United States' treatment of Spain in general as lenient. The top administrator for the islands' premier repository for government archives and historical manuscripts, Robertson interpreted the treaty broadly and in such a way as would allow for the institution's acquisition of a great deal of material. While Robertson's case for the colonial government's acquisition of materials from the Archives of Spain was historical—he appealed with his assessment that Filipinos were interested in the material—his argument relied upon the peace treaty that had ended the Spanish-American War. In other words, Robertson's argument for the resources to support scholarship on the history of a people, an unmistakable project of the United States' civil government in the Philippines, depended on the United States' successful military occupation of the Philippines.

By the time Robertson wrote his letter to the Philippine Commission's Executive Secretary in 1912, the purpose of the Spanish archives in the entrenchment of the new American regime was less clear than it had been just a decade earlier. In early reports, the military occupation and establishment of civil rule loomed in the narratives about the archives. In the Report of the Chief of the Bureau of Archives, included in the Philippine Commission Report of 1901, for example, Manuel Yriarte explained his bureau's early effort to bring all the records dispersed throughout the offices of the Spanish government into the Intendencia Building. Yriarte noted that such records were valuable not only for their historical information, but for their use in "the formation and administration of laws relating to the Filipino people." [31] Despite his bureau's earnest efforts to consolidate the voluminous records of the Spanish government, they were nonetheless thwarted by soldiers who, unaware of the papers' special value, used them "for fuel in the preparation of their food or threw them into the streets."[32] The purposes of the archive—some desirable in Yriarte's eyes, others not—were basic to the foundation of the project of United States occupation.

While the language of the Treaty of Paris clauses pertaining to the United States' acquisition of the Spanish regime's administrative records was broad, colonial administrators—holdovers from the Spanish regime and, later, recent American arrivals—found that the records ceded from Spain were in poor condition. Of course, these archives were not perceived to be the most valuable concessions from the Spanish Crown per se, but as Worthington Chauncey Ford and James Alexander Robertson would depict it, paying serious and proper attention to them was crucial to the writing of historical accounts of the colonies and the Spanish empire, as well as to the United States' successful administration of its new colonies. In other words, though archives were not immediately and obviously the most valuable of war booty, such as arable land and mining concessions and harbors and ports, they were important for understanding the development of these more valuable elements under the Spanish regime, and under the Americans, for their new administration. It was to this conception of the United States' enterprises in the Philippines that, taken together, Ford and Robertson appealed.

In the United States, both Ford and Robertson enjoyed some currency, as far as their evaluations of archives were concerned. Worthington Chauncey Ford descended from a family that had settled in New England in 1623 and, though he did not complete his degree at Columbia University, he nevertheless enjoyed a bookish life and social standing that gave him positions in the United States State Department and Treasury Department as a young man. Ford later worked at the Boston Public Library and at the time he wrote about the condition of public records in the United States' colonies, he was employed in the Division of Manuscripts at the Library of Congress.[33]

James Alexander Robertson, the first director of the Philippine Library, began his career as a proofreader at the Burrows Brothers Publishing Company in Cleveland, Ohio. He later moved to Madison, Wisconsin, where he began his collaboration with Emma Helen Blair on *The Philippine Islands, 1493-1898*. That project required Robertson to visit institutions holding material on the Spanish rule of the Philippines during extended stays in Europe between 1902 and 1907, which would inform his later scholarly works and position him well to acquire materials for the Philippine Library.[34] Whereas Ford established himself with a career in the United States, Robertson did the same for himself in the Philippines. Taken together, their assessment of the conditions of archives in the Philippines would have been accepted as authoritative.

At the annual meeting of the American Historical Association in 1904, Worthington Chauncey Ford delivered a paper, "Public Records in Our Dependencies," on the past, present, and future of archives acquired by the United States per treaties with Spain signed throughout the nineteenth century.[35] Citing articles of those treaties that related to records, Ford began from the premise that one could reasonably assume that there would be a wealth of documentation for historians. What followed, however, was not a discussion of the rich historical record, but of why public records were indeed so incomplete and in disarray.

To varying degrees, Britons, Americans, and Spaniards were all responsible for the physically disarrayed and intellectually incomplete public records in the

Philippines. During the British occupation of the islands between 1762 and 1764, Spanish colonial records were transferred to the British Museum. In the first months of the American occupation, United States soldiers, in their need to make space for themselves inside the colonial administration's buildings, destroyed records that they mistakenly believed to be without value. Even during times of relative peace under the Spanish regime, public records did not receive proper care. Ford attributed this improper care to the Philippines' tropical environment wherein insects and mold were a physical menace to the records and, in keeping with the era's racialized notion that whites' physical constitution made them ill-disposed to working in tropical climates, to the indifference of Spanish colonial bureaucrats whom Ford alleged were unable to work at full capacity due to the Philippines' environment.

While Ford's report on the condition of archives acquired by the United States per treaty with Spain primarily focused on the physical condition and the extent and scope of the public records, he also spoke to their evidentiary value. For example, Ford pointed to the ways that the spoils system would affect the content of the colonial state's records.

> The laws of the Indies were in their day a monument of administrative industry, but it was one thing to pass a law and another to carry it into effect. The colonies were distant, close supervision difficult, the agent spoilsmen, and the natives were to be exploited. The mass of decrees and dispatches indicate that there was weakness somewhere in the chain, and hence this great mass is needed for a corrective. The good or the ill wishes of the home government were embodied in the decree; the application of the wish and the results would be recorded in the report of the colonial administration. If a rosy view dominates in the actual message from the governor-general to his official superiors on whose favor his office and profits depended, a corrective exists in the local and provincial reports, also prepared by those anxious to please the higher powers, but written at a so much closer range as to be deprived of a certain tropical exuberance that gave a pictorial effect to the summary.[36]

Thus, in identifying three classes of records—decrees and dispatches, reports of the governor-general, and reports of local and provincial officials—Ford made clear why a greater and more comprehensive body of records would facilitate a more complex, and likely more accurate, understanding of the Spanish colonial state. The local and provincial reports record the problems, the governor-general reports minimize the problems, and the laws outline their resolution as they also further delineate the shape of the problems. While all parties involved in the production of these records have a vested interest in projecting "a certain tropical exuberance," if their records could be read alongside each other, another picture may emerge. However, the incompleteness of the records meant that such an analysis was merely a dashed possibility.

As telling as Ford's assessment of the incompleteness of certain classes or series of Spanish colonial archives was his evaluation of the records that possibly were complete.

> The larger mass of papers was naturally of a purely administrative character, bureau and departmental reports, and documents, local, municipal, and provincial. The nature as well as the arrangement of these papers forbade a close examination of any branch of them. To strike a number of formal returns, the stubs of public documents issued, or a package of minute items not unlike the individual returns made to our census was too discouraging.[37]

The above excerpt refers to the sorts of records that, by Ford's own estimation, presented the most clear and accurate accounts of conditions in the Philippines. Indeed they were a considerable volume of material, but they also present a range of types and originating offices—reports and documents of bureaus and departments, and of local, municipal, and provincial offices. Their "purely administrative" nature and prohibitive arrangement suggests that the labor required to review them was not worthwhile. In short, though Ford himself concluded that such mundane records would be useful for understanding the Spain's colonial government in the Philippines, he did not conduct a close examination of any of them.

Assessment of these records, theoretically valuable for precisely their minuteness, was prevented by the volume that necessarily defined them. This aspect of Ford's assessment of the Spanish archives ceded to the United States per the Treaty of Paris would recur throughout the administration of the Bureau of Archives under American rule. The records whose volume and nature was "too discouraging" both served the colonial state in their primary and explicitly stated sense—documenting local legislation, for example, or as would be the case in 1905, tabulating the islands' first census—but the discouragement they inspired also served the colonial state by dissuading close and careful observation and, thus, also curbing critique.

Ford concluded that "The problem which constantly meets us in dealing with records is the reasons for their incompleteness. Apparently, under a government largely military and strongly centralized, possessing a centripetal energy that drew to certain places the activities of the outlying administrative regions, the material has disappeared."[38] Tacit in Ford's final assessment was that, under the new American regime, these conditions would be corrected. This would be evidenced in the United States' negotiations with the religious orders to remove remaining friars from the islands, the promise of improved and efficient government administration, and even the introduction of modern methods to protect the archives that happened to have survived the centuries. Thus, in outlining how the "public records in our dependencies" would seem to be, how they were in fact, and how they might be under United States control, Ford's report to the American Historical Association promoted—in its modest way, but in keeping with popular imperialist views—the benefits of United States rule in the Philippines, as well as Guam and Puerto Rico.

Five years later, James Alexander Robertson's "Notes on the Archives of the Philippines" provided an update to Ford's report with a focus on the Philippines.[39] While the utility of Spanish colonial records to the United States' administration of the Philippines may have been inferred from Ford's 1904 report, its focus on the disorder resulting from war featured more centrally. By 1910, however, major hostilities between Philippine and United States forces had concluded, and officials in the United States were focused on the efficiency of its colonial administration. Robertson's report reflects the shift in concern from military occupation to civil administration.

Indeed, the Americans had become what Ford had, just a few years earlier, had said of the Spanish: "The Spanish official was created to prepare reports, and in the dependencies of Spain this function received a cultivation that borders upon excess. It is possible, perhaps, to picture the first comers with sword in hand; their successors took to the pen."[40] Moreover, Robertson was the consummate historian-bureaucrat, having made a name for himself with his scholarship on the Philippines and making a life for himself as a division head in the United States' colonial administration. These differences—between the concerns raised by military occupation and civil administration, between an American based at the Library of Congress and an American based at the Philippine Library—are neatly encapsulated by Robertson's opening comments, which in turn, set the tone for his report on the state of archives in his care.

Robertson introduced his report on the conditions of archives in the Philippines with the observation that while the United States had acquired the Spanish archives on the Philippines per treaty, just as it had done in the cases of East Florida, New Mexico and California, the archives in the Philippines distinguished themselves as the collection that ought to stay at its originating location, rather than be transferred to the Library of Congress. The impressive volume of these records, which Robertson estimated to be more than 5,000,000 pages, may have accounted in part for the distinction; more probably, the case for their staying in the Philippines rested on the fact that they were a "decidedly active asset at the present time in land questions and other matters which are productive of lawsuits."[41] Robertson posited that the archives' primary importance was utility to colonial administration.

Two other aspects of Robertson's report on the archives of the Philippines deserve mention, as they enjoyed especial currency throughout the first two decades of United States rule. First, the report dutifully details the poor physical condition of the archives, noting that many documents "have been destroyed through the wanton fortune of war, by the insect pests so much to be dreaded out here, and by the tropical climate which is so hostile to the preservation of documents."[42] Throughout the first two decades of United States colonial rule of the Philippines, the sorry state of the archives was a consistent theme in reports from the Bureau of Archives to the Philippine Commission. The stated reasons for this were invariably reported as the inadequate storage facilities and the ignorance of soldiers. The tacit reason was the ineptitude of the previous administration, which found expression whether United States officials were discussing the economy of the Philippines, public health and education, or central administration.

The second noteworthy aspect of Robertson's report both complements and contradicts the assessment of the archives' conditions. More precisely, Robertson is careful to note that the colonial government's archivist, Manuel Yriarte, is "almost entirely Spanish in blood" and that "The Filipinos appreciate thoroughly the importance of preserving these priceless records, and Americans are bringing enlightened means to bear for their future care."[43] Thus, while the maintenance and operation of the archives necessitated the continued employment of Manuel Yriarte, they would only be fully appreciated when the work of the Spaniard was brought under the "enlightened means" of the Americans. This formulation—Spanish ineptitude replaced by American ingenuity for Filipino benefit—was one that enjoyed considerable currency throughout the years of United States rule in the Philippines. Its ready application to the archival spoils of war was clear in Robertson's report in 1910, as well as in his later reports as Director of the Philippine Library.

Ford and Robertson demonstrate that in the first years of the United States' occupation of the Philippines, the administration of archives ceded by Spain faced the same challenges as did nearly every other of Spain's cessions to the United States. That is, once having won control of the archives from previous colonial administration, what were the Americans to do? Negotiating for the transfer of ownership was just the beginning.

Between 1910 and 1916, historian James Alexander Robertson was Director of the Philippine Library. Having completed the publication of his and Emma Helen Blair's *The Philippine Islands, 1493-1898*, a 55-volume compilation of documents from European archives relating to the Philippine Islands along with English translations, in 1907, officials in the United States colonial administration of the Philippines deemed Robertson authoritative enough to merit appointment to the islands' major public library. As perhaps ought to have been expected given his previous experience, Robertson's attention quickly turned to the acquisition of additional historical manuscript material for the library's Filipiniana division.

The means by which the Philippine Library could acquire such material, Robertson reasoned, was through Article VIII of the Treaty of Paris that referred to the transfer or reproduction of Spanish documents relating to the administration of the Philippines. This proposed route of acquisition ultimately placed some strain on the library's relationship with the Bureau of Insular Affairs and demanded careful attention to the meaning and limits of Article VIII of the treaty. The article pertaining to archives allowed for the cession or reproduction of records that, in whole or in part, referred to the sovereignty of the islands in the archives of Spain. Likewise, if any ceded records pertained to the sovereignty of Spain, the United States would make them available to the ousted regime.

In the letter to the Governor-General on May 10, 1912, noted above, Robertson noted that the archives of Spain held "thousands of documents relating to the Philippines," and Clemente J. Zulueta, collecting Librarian for the Government of the Philippine Islands, had collected only "a few hundred of these documents."[44] Robertson believed that the colonial government had right to receive more such documents or copies thereof at the expense of the Spanish Government, noting that if such transfer had been lackadaisically pursued in the past, "now is the time to cause enforcement."[45]

Analyzing both the treaty and Robertson's right to request the transfer or reproduction of materials in Spanish archives to the Philippine Library, Chief of the Division of Archives Manuel Yriarte highlighted the fact that Spain needed only to provide copies from the archives *upon request*. Further, he observed that the Philippine Commission's appointment of Clemente Zulueta to Collecting Librarian in 1903 to procure copies of historical manuscripts addressed the government's desire for documents not directly relating to the administration of the islands and, therefore, obviated the need for Robertson's requests. In conclusion, Yriarte wrote that he did "not believe that obtaining copies of such documents just to enrich libraries may be considered for official uses."[46]

After circulation throughout the colonial government in the Philippines and the metropolitan government in the United States, Robertson's general request did not make its way to the highest Spanish authorities. Rather, he was asked to provide a more specific list of materials he desired for the Philippine Library, which he did in November 1912. Robertson's case for the acquisition of these Spanish archives was undeniably and unapologetically historical in nature, noting that the leniency with which the Spanish and Philippine governments dealt with the colonial archives "should not extend to the voluntary relinquishment of documents that are so valuable for the history of the Philippine Islands, and which are in great part mere dead material in the Archives of Spain."[47]

When Robertson's request for materials from the archives of Spain arrived in Washington, however, the Bureau of Insular Affairs did not receive it kindly. Forwarding Robertson's letter to a subordinate at the BIA for review, bureau chief Frank McIntyre wrote plainly that:

> This request from the P.I. comes in such bad shape that it is difficult to put it into intelligent form. We should not forward propositions that would only embarrass our Minister. If there is something we want, it should be specifically described and our right to it made reasonably clear; if we have no right we should make clear why we request it as a favor. Half baked requests for an entire library will receive no consideration. Have someone examine these papers and see what is wanted, whether we are entitled to it and if not why we want it.[48]

Review of Robertson's request concluded that his case for the transfer or reproduction of records should not be forwarded, because the materials he sought were not of administrative value. However compelling his case for their historical value, which indeed was the value upon which Robertson made his point, such a measure did not merit the attention of American and Spanish diplomats. Indeed, as the internal memoranda illustrate, Robertson's persistence seemed to grate on the administration at the Bureau of Insular Affairs. Thus, again, Roberton's request was denied.

The final comments of McIntyre on the matter provide a concise explanation of why. He noted "an indispensable condition to establish our right to these papers is to show that they have an administrative value and are needed in our administration of the affairs of the Philippines Islands," and he further noted:

> Robertson has laid particular stress on their historical value but there is nothing to show that they are really needed for administrative purposes. It is doubtless true that the documents would be a valuable acquisition from

an historical standpoint but at the same time might not the question be well asked—Are they not as valuable to the Spanish Government, and would it be fair to ask the Spanish Government to deprive itself of data covering history-making epochs?[49]

If the records were not administratively useful to the United States' governing of the Philippines, then Spain had an equal claim to them.

***

In 1904 and 1910, Ford and Robertson indicated how the clauses of the treaty that addressed the cession of archives from Spain to the United States were important for the colonial administration of the islands. It was obscured somewhat in the decade after as Robertson—newly appointed director of the Philippine Library—sought to increase that institution's holdings. The three interests in tension in these instances of interpreting the archives clauses and evaluating Spain's and the United States' efforts to adhere to the conditions of those clauses are apparent. They figured centrally in reports of the United States' administration in the Philippines. First, the attention to archives in the Treaty of Paris established the archives as part of negotiations to end the war and thus, indicated the archives as an institutional prize to be won in conquest.

Second, when questions of how much of the archives Spain was obliged to reproduce or outright cede to the United States were raised, the argument that the archives were not just a trophy of war, but also as an administrative necessity, gained currency. Related to this, the archives were read to document, in the esteem of Americans, an inadequate, inefficient, and corrupt Spanish colonial system that would serve as a foil for the United States' purportedly benevolent, efficient, and modern system of colonial governance. Finally, the arguments for the care of archives as important for the historical study of Spanish colonialism by Americans and, later, for the historical study of the Philippines by both Filipinos and Americans underscored their role in crafting national identity.

In short, the Treaty of Paris to end the Spanish-American War was a significant event. It not only ended hostilities between an empire in decline and an empire in ascension, but it also transferred for twenty million dollars, Spain's colonial territories to the United States. The drama and excitement of the war was concluded, and negotiating the loot was the business at hand. Arable land, ports and harbors, mines, forests—these assets of the Philippines and the promise of their exploitation quickly drew the attention of both proponents and opponents of annexation.

The clauses in the Treaty of Paris that dealt with the transfer of archives also addressed the transfer of immovable property such as buildings and other colonial government structures in the islands. Without a doubt, these were the least spectacular of the United States' gains, but their deliberate treatment in the peace agreement indicate their importance to the administration of the islands' agricultural and forest lands, as well as their waterways. In other words, these facilities and archives—however inadequate Ford, Robertson, and Yriarte would report them to be—were crucial to the development of the bigger prizes of the Spanish-American War. The changes to the administration of land under the United States' regime, for example, was supposed to demonstrate the marked improvement of the governance from what islanders experienced under the Spaniards. The greatest projects of the civil government owed their existence to the negotiations to end a military conflict.

Still, reports of the armed occupation of the islands would come to be drowned out by reports of the successes of "benevolent assimilation." The origins of successful colonial projects—such as the construction of trails and roads, the improvement of ports and harbors, the establishment of public schools and health clinics—had origins in the military occupation, and in some instances, served to ease the transition from military to civilian rule. However, to trace the continuity of the promise of disciplinary violence and to consider how this violent promise animated the civil administration, the changing interpretations of clauses of the Treaty of Paris pertaining to archives are especially instructive because questions about the archives always referred back to the treaty that ended the Spanish-American War. With this invariable referent in these early discussions, the archives' martial origins were unmistakable, even though the archives were those of the Spanish colonial bureaucracy. Equally unmistakable was the necessity of archives in times of war, and in the preparation for war's end, as consideration of John R.M Taylor's compilation and translation of Philippine government documents—captured in the Philippines and sent to the United States Department of War's Bureau of Insular Affairs—attests.

John R.M. Taylor's *Compilation of Philippine Insurgent Records*

> "I had this book of official stamped paper of the Philippine Insurgent Government bound in Manila twenty years ago without any particular intention of using it. Now I have decided to use it as a note book—a commonplace book in the old term I think—in which to note references to books read and to conversations heard which seem worth recording. It would have been an interesting record if I had begun it in 1900 but there may be something yet if I

fill these pages. At any rate I shall try."[50]

Amidst the upheaval of the continuing Philippine Revolution and the Philippine-American War, John R.M. Taylor, army officer and editor of *Compilation of Philippine Insurgent Records*, had the stationary of the Philippine Revolutionary Government bound into a neat volume that has survived the twentieth century and remains housed in the Manuscript Division of the Library of Congress in Washington, D.C. The above quote is Taylor's introduction to his journal that covers, as promised, "books read" and "conversations heard," beginning in 1921.

That Taylor tidily bound his souvenirs of war into a book, that his observations in this book are made on the stationary of an ousted revolutionary government, that his "commonplace book" covers his everyday, everyman observations after he and his staff worked to compile and translate the records of the Philippine Revolutionary Government—these matters of fact provide an illustration as neat as bound, blank stationary of how the archives of war could be so readily and easily incorporated into the pedestrian business of colonial governance.

An important aspect of American evaluations of the revolutionary government turned on how closely the Filipinos approximated the United States' models of governance. Of course, the drafting of a constitution, the circulation of decrees, and the official appeals to United States representatives in the both the United States and the Philippines were all practical measures to advocate for the revolutionary government and demonstrate capacity for Filipino self-government. Also, they required stationary, which Taylor idly gathered up and brought back to the United States.

What makes this example so neat, of course, is that though Taylor used the actual stationary of the revolutionary government as the pages of his commonplace book in 1921, with his responsibility for the compilation, translation and annotation of seized government records for readers in the United States, the seized documents functioned anyway as his blank stationary. Beginning in 1899, commanding officers at United States military posts throughout the archipelago were required to send reports to the Military Governor on the condition of archives in the area they occupied. Also, soldiers were mandated to transfer found records to the central administration for review.

Despite the fact that many records were lost in the course of war, Captain John R.M. Taylor nevertheless had approximately three tons of documents at his disposal. By 1905, Taylor had reviewed over 12,000 items. Concerns about the political wisdom of publishing Taylor's work as William Howard Taft campaigned for the office of the President of the United States, as well as an unfavorable review from James LeRoy, resulted in the indefinite postponement of the compilation's publication.[51] Consideration of the efforts to collect, translate and publish the Philippine Revolutionary Government's records, and the challenges that attended those efforts, suggest how seriously the United States took the archives even while waging a war. In fact, Taylor's work was unpublished during his lifetime and only saw a broader readership when it was edited by Philippine scholar Renato Constantino of the Eugenio Lopez Museum.[52]

The United States' recognition of the importance of the records of the Philippine Revolutionary Government was immediately apparent, as the creation of the Office of Insurgent Records was mandated in the first special order of the Office of the United States Military Governor in the Philippines in 1900. Beginning with naming the office as the Office of Insurgent Records, the United States demonstrated a clear, vested interest in de-legitimizing the newly-established Philippine Republic. By insisting that the revolution was an insurgency, the Americans situated the United States as the rightful sovereign of the islands and framed the work and aspirations of Filipino nationalists as in unjust conflict with the rule of law. The Office of Insurgent Records was charged with "the classification and translation of captured insurgent records," many of which related "mainly to the military operations of the insurgents and the operation of such governments, municipal and central, as were set up and conducted by them."[53] Some of the records reviewed by this office would eventually be those included in *Compilation of Philippine Insurgent Records*.

As the director of the compilation project administered through the Department of War's Bureau of Insular Affairs, Captain John R.M. Taylor was the point of contact for government officials in the United States and the Philippines who sought primary source information on the war. In 1902, for example, Taylor provided Senator Dietrich (R-Nebraska) with a report on "the more prominent Filipino leaders at the beginning of the Philippine insurrection and the acts by which they are best known."[54] Four years later, after the controversy surrounding the compilation's publication, Taylor would still be reviewing the documents held in the Office Insurgent Records for his commanding officer, Chief of Bureau of Insular Affairs Clarence Ransom Edwards.[55] The enormous volume of the records and the understaffing of the office made it impossible to maintain intellectual control over the documents. Thus, in 1908, though at least two employees of the office had laid eyes on every document to come into United States' possession, a complete index of the captured materials was, nearly a decade after the first records were acquired, an impossibility.[56]

The challenges facing the Office of Insurgent Affairs were numerous and considerable, given that its charge was three-fold: to collect, translate, and circulate records received. The first of these challenges was the simple acquisition of records and their unmolested transfer from the Philippines to the United States. Sometimes illegible records would arrive at the Office of Insurgent Records, making it impossible to translate or publish them.[57]

A second challenge was hiring and retaining capable translators and gaining access to dictionaries and grammars to facilitate translation. With so few Americans proficient in any of the languages of the Philippines, the translation of captured documents was likely very arduous. This translation relied on access to dictionaries, either on loan from the Library of Congress, Augustinian Friars in the islands, or the Philippine Constabulary's Division of Information.[58] Filipino records in Spanish, of course, were far more accessible to Americans, and the records of the Bureau of Insular Affairs evidence the hiring and retention of these documents' translators.[59]

A third challenge was the prohibitive cost of publishing the documents. The Deficiency Act of 1905, for example, limited the publication of federal government documents, and other efforts at economy rendered the compilation less of a priority. Even the modest expense of printing the compilation in galley proof did not escape the notice of the Office of Insurgent Records' superiors.[60]

The final challenge was neither logistical nor financial, but plainly political. This challenge was the most formidable and most telling. As late as 1908, Chief of Bureau of Insular Affairs Frank McIntyre candidly wrote to James A. LeRoy, former secretary to Dean C. Worcester and an historian of the Philippines, that "Captain Taylor's compilation has not yet been published, and it begins to look as though it never would be."[61] Controversy attended Taylor's introductory chapter to the compilation to such a degree that Secretary of War William Howard Taft was enlisted to revise the statement, though in fact, according to Clarence Ransom Edwards, he never saw it. Taft noted that, "I am a good deal concerned in reference to the propriety of publishing at public expense a history that gives so many opinions as Taylor's resume does, and I feel, therefore, that I must go over it with a great deal more care, in order to eliminate the expression of opinion, than under ordinary circumstances."[62] And Taylor seemed well aware of his political mis-steps that resulted in the compilation's deferred publication, when he wrote to Clarence Edwards that "I have always been rather afraid that the Secretary of War would find that I had said a good deal that he did not consider expedient to publish and therefore I was not willing to print 'The Philippine Insurrection Against the United States' until he had gone over the galley proofs."[63]

In addition to Secretary of War Taft, James A. LeRoy, W. Cameron Forbes, Luke E. Wright, and perhaps others received the proofs as well.[64] Taft's reservations did not necessarily mean that Taylor's introduction was especially critical of the United States' relations with the Philippine Revolutionary Government. LeRoy mentioned to James A. Robertson that Taylor's work "was even worse than I had feared, both in editing of documents and in his 'historical' chapters," going so far as to say that he hoped the "the result will be the postponement and entire revision."[65] In 1909, the compilation remained unpublished. Chief Edwards' written request to Governor-General Luke E. Wright for permission to publish Taylor's work provides the most complete account of the work of the Office of Insurgent Records and the reasons for the compilation's deferred publication. This deferral may have tarnished Taylor's reputation somewhat, even as Edwards explained

> as a trained and experienced officer, an active participant in the Spanish War and Philippine insurrection, familiar with many of the incidents and scenes to which these documents refer, and possessing a wide acquaintance with the people producing them, together with a knowledge not only of Spanish but of local dialects, his fitness for the work designed seemed assured.[66]

Edwards also explained some of the reasons why it made sense to publish the insurgent records presently, but not previously. He noted that it would not have been wise to publish the revolutionary papers before the United States' benevolent intentions were adequately impressed upon the native population, and that likewise, it would have been unwise to publish the papers while elections were taking place in the United States. This reasoning revealed political wisdom, as the compilation included precisely the kinds of government documents that Filipinos allegedly were incapable of writing. These included, of course, circulars and memoranda pertaining to the establishment of a civil government independent of the Spanish regime.

The Would-Be Government Archives of the first Philippine Republic

Though neither comprehensive nor necessarily representative, the Philippine government documents that Taylor and his staff compiled and translated were nevertheless the primary sources upon which Americans would have relied for information about the constitution and actions of the revolutionary government. The operative phrase here is "would have," again, because Taylor's work was unpublished until 1971. The translations were accessible to the staff of the Bureau of Insular Affairs, others in the War Department, and officials in the United States' military and, later, civil governments in the Philippines. In the throes of war, these government officers were likely paying closest attention to the translations pertaining to the Philippine forces' movements and guerilla strategies and taking less seriously the Philippine government's decrees and instructions on recordkeeping. Still, mixed in with these more urgently needed documents were those that outlined why good records were needed while hostilities between United States and Philippine forces continued, and that outlined the bureaucratic shape and mundane operations of the Philippine government that would be realized, once the war was won.

The Philippine documents pertaining to recordkeeping and archives are significant for a consideration of the United States colonial government's archives for a few reasons. They indicate that recordkeeping was important for particular aspects of the war effort (supplies, political and financial support), in spite of the fact that the loss of records and their collection or seizure by Americans threatened to compromise that effort. Also, they suggested what the government would look like once the war was won, including descriptions of the various departments. This is important both for understanding what the Filipinos were trying to achieve and for appreciating that the formulation of such a structure was part of the project to exhibit capacity for self-government. Finally, they show how similarly some of these departments would be structured, under Filipinos or Americans, when the Americans self-legitimating line was that they were able to bring good, modern government to Filipinos.

The Philippine government documents compiled and translated by Taylor relating to the care and maintenance of records may themselves be categorized. One class addresses the creation of records or inventorying of existing Spanish records relating to property that would be of short- or long-term use to the government. Another relates to the demographics of those not directly involved in combat with Americans. A third class relates to the proper routing of records through official government channels, speaking both to the immediate needs of the military government and the shape of the bureaucracy once hostilities with the United States subsided. A fourth class addresses historical records directly. Taken together, these documents illustrate the varied and invariably significant roles that recordkeeping played in the Philippine government, both for the everyday business of governance and for the demonstration of Filipino capacity for self-rule.

Whether it was through the generation of new materials or inventorying of existing Spanish documents, records that accounted for abandoned or seized property were important for the continuation of the Philippines' struggle against the United States. Such records would not only suggest the monetary value of property with long-term use for the Philippine government, but more importantly, they would suggest the ways that such property—whether arms and ammunition or a safe place to bunker—could be used for the immediate needs of the armed struggle. These were complemented by circulars that offered guidelines and instruction for the collection of taxes from non-combatants in support of hostilities against the United States. While the primary purpose for the uniformity of the records that accounted for property and income was to gain an accurate financial picture for the Philippine government during the war, the mandates to gather these records centrally would be helpful in the immediate aftermath of war, and would eventually constitute the core of a government's archive.

As early as May 24, 1898, more than two weeks before the proclamation of Philippine independence from Spanish rule, notes attributed to Emilio Aguinaldo on the establishment of the Provisional Government of the Philippines included a part that ordered that "All property hereafter seized from the enemy must be recorded or entered in an inventory made by the municipal captain and the officers of the Tribunal (members of the Municipal Board), and same shall be considered as the property of the Provisional Government of the Philippines" and, further, that "All records and documents, such as tax books, etc., shall be properly kept."[67] Later letters of instruction to military commanders and provincial presidents specified that these inventories should be made of seized rifles, and others of "the amount of money, number of animals, and other property seized from the enemy", and "all the property left by the Spaniards, in cash as well as in kind and live stock."[68] In a document dated May 19, 1900, the importance of these materials and inventories was underscored by the threat of death:

> You, Captain Antonio and Judge Cornelio must perfectly understand what this order says; when the wealthy are Americanistas, you must seize all their money, clothing and other property belonging to them, immediately making an inventory of the property seized, and you may remain in the place where the seizure is made as long as may be necessary to make said inventory, even though a great amount is spent for maintenance.
>
> Know furthermore, that if the soldiers take any of the property seized, they will speedily be put to death and will surely go to hell; therefore, when it becomes necessary to enter a town to make a seizure, you must direct the soldiers not to touch the goods seized, even the most insignificant, in order to avoid consequences of this character.[69]

By the time of this order, the Spanish-American War had ended and the Philippine-American War had begun. As Spaniards left the islands or pledged their allegiance — either to Spain or to the United States — and Americans were poised to establish a civil government, the treatment of people sympathetic to the United States' project, "Americanistas," grew severe. Such treatment—namely the seizure of "all their money, clothing, and other property belonging to them"—served not only to set an example for others of what would result from such sympathies, but just as importantly, the treatment materially aided the Philippines forces in its ongoing warring with the United States.

While the extant records of the Philippine government that were seized, compiled, and translated by the United States do not happen to contain the inventories resulting from the above order or any other, and the United States' eventual military victory over the Philippine Republic resolved the question of what would have been the course of that government's military records, it is important to consider this question of "what would have." This is a worthwhile pause, because the Philippine government's beginning steps, as demonstrated by these orders, suggests that its later steps might have paralleled those taken by the United States. The United States' forces did just as the Philippine forces, insofar as they seized and inventoried materials from opposing forces and non-combatants. (Indeed, Taylor's five-volume work of compilation and translation was made possible by such seizures.) These materials presumably included more than food and clothing, as buildings that were occupied or money that was confiscated would require disposition when the war was over. As it so happened, with the United States' military triumph, this disposition facilitated the establishment and entrenchment of the colonial government. This facilitation would be especially evident with regard to the seizure, inventorying, and disposition of land.

For the Philippine government, the inventories generated by its military forces served the immediate needs in fighting a war with the United States, but after the war—having served their primary purpose—would have been used for the sorting out of goods and property under the new republic. If these early orders of the Philippine government—first provisional and later first republic—indicate the immediate and material necessity to both seize and inventory arms, ammunition, money and animals, a parallel series of documents that appertain to the lands of the archipelago suggested officials' foresight about the government's needs once the hostilities with Spain and, later, the United States, subsided.

Writing to officials in Batangas on June 11, 1898, for example, Emilio Aguinaldo wrote that "Whereas this Government is still in a state of organization and all its efforts are to secure the welfare of the Philippines, I deem it wise to advise all Local Chiefs to protect all titles to estates and not to consider any claim which would seem to disturb their owners in the peaceful possession of such estate."⁷⁰ Shortly after the establishment of the Philippine Republic, on November 30, 1898, the new government decreed the introduction of instruments and procedures in transactions pertaining to land with the aim of avoiding and correcting "fraudulent transactions."⁷¹ This decree placed the power of selling land to Spaniards and other foreigners in the hands of the Office of the President and ordered instruments and contracts not approved by that office "null and void."⁷² Implicit in this decree was that the upheaval of the ongoing revolution and the goal of correcting the concentration of land and wealth in the hands of Spaniards necessitated the introduction of an entirely new system of recording land tenure and justified the annulment of land titles claimed outside of the Philippine government's jurisdiction.

By February 27, 1899, the recently established Office of the Secretary of Agriculture, Industry and Commerce distributed "Regulations for the Adjudication of Uncultivated Lands, which have not yet passed into private ownership, or cultivated lands the ownership of which it is desired to acquire."⁷³ This document not only included a detailed listing of the requirements to acquire land. It also included several forms—which asked for the applicant's name, profession, listing of relatives, and physical descriptions of the desired lands—that upon receipt in the Office of the Secretary of Agriculture, Industry and Commerce and subsequent approval, would be filed on government record and subsequently published in the government's official news organ. Thus, in the midst of war, the Philippine government was creating and circulating the public instruments by which it would eventually record the extent of the land of the archipelago and the demographics of its inhabitants.

A series of records suggest that the formal and systematic gathering of information about the people of the Philippines was not just incidental to the registration of land. Rather, there are indications that even at the height of hostilities with Spain and the United States, the Philippine government sought to compile a reliable register of the people. Instructions to municipal and provincial officials detailed where and how births, deaths, and marriages ought to be recorded.⁷⁴ Casualties of war also necessitated keeping records on people. Such recordkeeping, of course, may have been useful for developing strategy for warfare, but it was also necessary to determine the payment to the families of soldiers who had been killed and soldiers who had been wounded in the fighting.⁷⁵ Indeed, the more comprehensive the registration of individuals, the better the government's sense of not only the numbers of potential supporters of the cause of independence, but also the numbers of individuals subject to *cedula* payment that, in turn, would support the cause of independence. In this sense, getting to know the population was as crucial as successful campaigns against the United States.

The Revolutionary Government's Secretary of the Treasury M. del Rosario addressed this connection in a communication to the head of the province of Pangisinan, detailing the kinds of registers that should be sent to Malolos:

> I believe that it is excusable to recommend to your zeal the importance that at the present moment is involved in the adoption of the above measures: for these must form the basis of my work in a branch that must be the chief sinew of our new-born Government and of our administration; and likewise I trust in the patriotism that distinguishes you hoping that, without causing any necessity for reminders, you will secure exact compliance with this circular, with all the peremptoriness and urgency that this matter demands.[76]

Thus, even as the war with the United States loomed, the Secretary of the Treasury emphasized the importance of maintaining orderly records. In this instance, Rosario made the understandable connection between such records, the administration of the new government, and appeals to the provincial officials' patriotism to underscore his desire for their compliance. This connection—between the creation and maintenance of records and the project of nation-building—was drawn repeatedly, and with good reason. An unsigned draft of "Bases of a Resolution for the Regulation of Official Communications Directed to the Local Authorities," for example, notes that

> For the better understanding of the rulings to be issued concerning this matter it would be well to publish forms for official orders and communications which shall serve as models, such as the most enlightened powers use, and so that there be not one more ground for our enemies saying that Filipinos have no governmental aptitude [...].[77]

Just as the property inventories helped with the immediate needs of the military forces, and as the civil registers helped with an understanding of the population, the Philippine Republic's departmental records kept the machinery of the new government in motion. They also marked the Philippine Republic as a bureaucracy and underscored the revolutionary forces' claims to the capacity for self-government.

Emilio Aguinaldo's purpose in distributing his June 27, 1898, instructions from Cavite, for example, was "to insure that in the future the conduct of administrative proceedings shall not mean the paralysis of public business, but, on the contrary, that it shall constitute the best guarantee of regularity, promptness and expedition in the execution of public service [...]."⁷⁸ These instructions described the offices of the central government, composed of four departments: Foreign Relations, War (which was constituted by four divisions: Campaign, Military Justice, Military Administration, Medical, and Public Works), Interior, and Treasury. Per these instructions, the latter two departments—Interior and Treasury—were charged with responsibilities that had previously fallen to military officers in the field and municipal and provincial officials. The Department of the Interior became responsible for, among other things, the civil registration and the poll, and the Treasury Department became responsible for, among other things, the registration of property and cattle.⁷⁹ Notably, when the Philippine government was ousted and the United States government installed, the new regime was structured similarly and the responsibilities of the departments of the Interior and Treasury roughly approximated those outlined by Aguinaldo.

The revolutionary government's recordkeeping did not entirely depart from the systems established by the Spanish colonial government, as it was impracticable to institute entirely new systems. The Philippine notarial law of 1898 drew upon several articles of the Spanish notarial law of 1889, and even allowed for the notarization of public instruments on paper of the Spanish government.⁸⁰ This allowance reflects the vagaries of war more than an affinity for Spanish colonial governance. At around this same time, the revolutionary government provided directions for the inspection of local authorities and their maintenance of records in their charge. Of course, these inspections, in turn, were documented in reports to be submitted to the central office.⁸¹

In addition to outlining the rather involved protocol for official transactions, the June 27, 1898, instructions explicitly note that "The officials in charge shall take care of the records of their respective divisions, arranging cases which are closed in numbered packages. The provincial and popular archives shall be in charge of the respective Chiefs, assisted by suitable personnel."⁸² Thus, two weeks after the Philippines' declaration of independence, the instructions for the creation of government archives were folded into the general orders to establish the central government's constituent departments. In fact, several of the documents that United States forces seized, compiled, and translated address the matter of historical documents.

When the Department of Fomento was established, its responsibilities were divided among three directors—one of public instruction, the second of public works, and the third of agriculture and industry. The director of public instruction was charged with the regulation of "the institutions of primary and secondary instructions, universities, archives and libraries, fine arts and special schools, geographical and statistical institute."[83] As the administrative structure of the Philippine government grew to include seven departments—Foreign Affairs, Interior, Treasury, War and Navy, Public Instruction, Communications and Public Works, and Agriculture, Industry and Commerce—the regulation of archives was removed from the specific charge of the director of public instruction. Instead, each department was ordered to maintain on staff "an archivist who shall have charge of the organization and management of the archives."[84] Thus, as the government planned for growth, the maintenance and final disposition of the government's records were no longer centralized, but the responsibility of each department of the new administration. One division in the Bureau of the General Staff of the Army was charged with "daily accounts of operations and compilation of the history of the army and of its Official Bulletin."[85]

There is a peculiar irony in examining these documents to trace the history of an archive, or in the case of Philippine revolutionary government, the would-be archive of that government. The translations were to aid the American war in the islands—most obviously by knowing the movements and locations of the revolutionary forces, but also by understanding the personalities, the rhetoric, and the alliances of forces. In some ways, it was clear what was being suppressed—one needs only look at the lofty language of liberation, slavery, imperialism, and honor to understand the appeals to the general population's sense of national becoming. Also suppressed was the creation of a government bureaucracy comprised of many familiarly named departments.

Conclusion

With the cession of Spanish colonial archives per the Treaty of Paris, the United States government owned a veritable trove of information on the colony. Though the colonial administration ultimately designed a larger and purportedly more modern system for maintaining and preserving records in the islands, the records acquired by clause VIII of the treaty provided the core from which the administration could build. Moreover, as the records of the outgoing colonial state, they had been generated and used and circulated with particular administrative purposes. These government records were to facilitate the establishment and operation of a new, American colonial state.

If the records of the Spanish colonial government were to be acquired by treaty negotiation, the records of the Philippine revolutionary government were to be acquired by seizure. As was the case with Spanish language documents, the Tagalog language documents required an office of translators within the Bureau of Insular Affairs in the Department of War. With the enlistment of Captain John R.M. Taylor to direct the editing and translation of captured revolutionary records began a project that highlighted several important aspects of the American war in the Philippines. The difficulty of seizing records of the revolutionary government underscored the unfamiliar and challenging terrain in the United States' latest theater of war, for the following reasons. The shortage of available and qualified translators suggested the degree to which the Philippines and its languages had been (at best) peripheral to the concerns of the United States in any practical way; the controversy of the compilation's publication reflect the ways that partisan politics in the United States figured into the circulation of information about the Philippines; and the critical review of the compilation by a burgeoning group of historians of the Philippines and Spain anticipated the questions about reliable sources—access to, translation and publication of—that would concern historians throughout the early decades of the twentieth century. These government records, the capture and translation of which were necessitated by the exigencies of the ongoing Philippine Revolution, were to aid in the war and occupation by United States forces.

The cession of Spanish archives pertaining to colonial administration and the capture of Filipino records pertaining to revolutionary government were of undeniable, explicit value to the United States' war in and occupation of the Philippines. The United States was no less assisted by the generation of monographs, newspaper and magazine articles, memoirs and pamphlets, and other coverage by authors either enthusiastic about, or at least friendly to, the United States' actions in the Philippines. The argument could be economic, about the solution that Asia offered to the American problem of "overproduction"; political, about the lessons in democracy that the United States was especially qualified to teach; or cultural, about the civilization that white men ought to at least try to share. In any case, Americans were never too far from a media that would express it. War correspondents in the Philippines, soldiers' letters home, and "armchair" experts on the islands all contributed to a body of writing that argued that the United States' occupation of the Philippines was necessary and just. Such a barrage was significant not only for people living in the opening decades of the twentieth century, trying to understand national and world events. These records would maintain significance for decades to follow.

The creation and maintenance of archives was an important element of the United States' war in the Philippines. Though the core of the archives was acquired per the Treaty of Paris that ended the Spanish-American War, the so-called Philippine Insurgent Papers—in terms of Captain John R.M. Taylor's work to compile and translate documents of the first Philippine Republic as well as the content of those documents—suggest that when the United States and Philippines were at war, archives and recordkeeping were not simply matters to consider after one side triumphed. They were matters of consequence as the fighting raged on.

When Taylor's work was finally widely published in 1971, Renato Constantino introduced the compilation with the observation that "There is no source, no matter how biased, that does not yield a bit of historical truth."[86] When considering Taylor's work and *The Philippine Insurrection against the United States*, "a bit of historical truth" about the relationship between archives and war emerges: The exigencies of war—that is, the conditions that prompted the seizure, compilation, and translation of the revolutionary government's documents—provide a glimpse into how the leadership of that revolutionary government envisioned the role of archives in an independent Philippine Republic. The United States' suppression of the Philippine documents that articulated that vision created a conspicuous kind of informational vacuum about conditions in the archipelago. Thus, where Philippine government documents that illustrated the role of archives and that demonstrated capacity for self-rule would have circulated to make an argument against annexation and occupation of the islands, there were instead the records of more, other Americans. The records that filled this informational vacuum are the subject of the next chapter.

CHAPTER 3
ARCHIVES AND ANTI-IMPERIALISM

"Dear Uncle Moorfield: You asked me to keep my mind open and come out here and see things for myself as they really are. This I have tried to do, but I must own up to having spent a great many hours a day reading the official records, and yet it is hard to read the reports of the work done here by the Commission and the Chiefs of the Departments and not be impressed with the earnestness with which they have undertaken the great and difficult task imposed upon them, and the success which has attended some very important and material parts of their effort."
--W. Cameron Forbes to Moorfield Storey, January 3, 1905[87]

Introduction

If the Civil War pitted brother against brother, the Philippine-American War and the establishment of the United States colonial government in the islands pitted, as the epigraph indicates, uncle against nephew. In 1905, W. Cameron Forbes arrived in the Philippines as head of the Department of Commerce and Police and also as a Philippine Commissioner. A businessman by trade, Forbes played an integral part in thinking through the railroad options in the Philippines and he eventually rose to the position of Governor-General. In the same year that Forbes arrived in the Philippines to embark on his colonial service career, Forbes' uncle Moorfield Storey, became president of the Anti-Imperialist League. With his strong anti-imperialist views Storey served as the President of the League for the duration of its existence, though he is better-known for his role as the first President of the National Association for the Advancement of Colored People (NAACP.) Over the course of his career in the Philippines, Forbes consulted volumes of official government records and saw to the production of voluminous records. Moorfield Storey, as president of the Anti-Imperialist League for more than fifteen years, was the leader of an organization most prolific in its critique of the United States' actions in the Philippines. They stood firmly on opposing sides: Forbes convinced of the considerable good that the United States was doing in the islands, and Storey certain that the American course was a flawed one.

Taking a long view of the effects of imperialist policy, of course, was not only cause for disagreement and sounding of alarms. The United States' policy in the Philippines influenced partisan politics. The presidential election of 1900, for example, prompted President of the National Civil Service Reform League and former Senator Carl Schurz to note that McKinley's vision of U.S. colonial rule in the Philippines was "bound to bring upon this republic evils infinitely more disgraceful and disastrous in their effects than anything that has been predicted as likely to result from McKinley's defeat."[88] It prompted others to appeal for the continued work of the Anti-Imperialist League and the independent efforts of its members.[89] And throughout the first years of the twentieth century, especially when it was unclear whether Taft would stay to govern the Philippines or return to the United States, the course of action in the islands seemed even more volatile. Understanding this variety of opinion requires an appreciation of not only the national and international political concerns of that period, but also the tradition of protest with which a particular group of "anti-imperialists" were aligned. Moreover, while the lofty question—of whether to build an empire or maintain a republic—was one that animated debate about whether the war was just, the pedestrian question of how to manage abrasive or conflicting personalities also factored into discussions about the United States and the Philippines. In short, what came to be known as the anti-imperialist movement was complex. This complexity and conflict resulted in the generation of an enormous body of material, a counter-balance to that generated by the United States government in time of war.

The conditions that characterized and circumscribed the creation of documentation about the United States' war in the Philippines succeeded in defining the terms of the recorded debate, but they did not stem the voluminous production. This chapter considers one example of the Philippine-American War's unofficial archive, namely the testimonies, books, pamphlets, and editorials, of the Anti-Imperialist League and others opposed to the United States' course in the Philippines. This body of material may be recast in the light of anti-imperialists' self-conscious recording of an alternative record on war atrocities in the Philippines.

National Issues

> "I do not mean to underestimate the villainy of Spanish administration, but it is only within your memory and mine that *we* became virtuous [and abolished slavery], and even yet—judging from what the papers have been recently reporting about the lynching and burning of negroes—have not even now become thoroughly accustomed to being virtuous."
>
> --Charles Parkhurst, 1898[90]

Though the question of how the United States ought to manage its relationship with the Philippines attracted considerable attention in the first decades of the twentieth century, other issues—pertaining to labor disputes, race relations, civil service reform, currency, and free trade—also demanded the attention of Americans. With all of these issues in play, the members of the Anti-Imperialist League had varied motivations for joining. Though they could agree to protest the United States' occupation of the Philippines, their views differed on other subjects. Unsurprisingly, such a composition gave rise to conflicts within the movement, as well as garnered the vocal disdain of the movement's opponents. William Howard Taft's scorn, for example, was unmistakable. He wrote, "The shrieks, for I think they can be criticized as nothing less, of the anti-imperialists in the last campaign, in light of the result, are likely to become part of the humor of American politics."[91]

Reverend Charles Parkhurst cited the United States' only very recent abolition of slavery and the subsequent rise of lynching to suggest that the United States was not necessarily well-equipped to annex and occupy the Philippines. By discussing virtue and lynching, Parkhurst is helpful for understanding the relationship between archives and war in the Philippines and, more specifically, between national issues and the generation of an alternate, anti-imperialist archive. For one, Parkhurst questioned whether the United States has virtue enough to justify taking the place of the Spanish colonial administration in the Philippines, given the United States' historical and current treatment of African Americans, makes use of the notion of progress. The more frequently posed question of that moment was: have Filipinos progressed enough to govern themselves? Parkhurst's statement suggested the question: have Americans progressed enough to govern others? In short, he employed the logical frame used to justify the United States' occupation of the Philippines to present an argument against the United States' course of action in the islands.

In so doing, Parkhurst used the analytical tools available to him—or at the very least, those with a considerable amount of currency in the fervor of war—to make a countering point. If this sermon shows how such a rhetorical move may be made with the notion of hard-won, slow-to-realize virtue, it also shows how recent domestic events could be harnessed to critique foreign policy. In 1898, when Parkhurst delivered his sermon, lynching in the United States was regular and widespread, demonstrative of a national, state-condoned method to maintain a particular racial hierarchy. Whereas the terror of lynching worked to uphold white supremacy over African Americans, and by extension—one was to suppose—to non-whites all over the globe, Parkhurst's take on the notion of virtue allows for an argument that the epidemic of lynching was precisely the reason the United States ought not to get involved in the Philippines.

That Parkhurst's example was lynching is notable, given the "red record" that was absent from the mainstream press. By 1899, Ida B. Wells had been working for years to identify and make a case for the fact that lynching was a national problem. She had taken two speaking tours through England, Scotland, and Wales to discuss the problem of lynching in the United States. She had also published two influential pamphlets, *Southern Horrors: Lynch Law in All Its Phases* and *A Red Record*, that compiled information about and detailed instances of lynching in the United States. Wells' project to aggregate information published in newspapers—white, mainstream, and therefore, indisputable—named a national crisis, creating a record of great import.[92] The alternative archive that was Wells' serial investigation of lynching in the United States provided both a model—using the sources or terms in ready circulation—and the content—the continued, indeed increasing, violence against African Americans—for Parkhurst's argument about the misguided United States policy in the Philippines. In addition to the publication (upon request) of Parkhurst's sermon, publications critical of the annexation of the Philippines and the American war in the islands were sometimes targeted to segments of the United States population that, for one reason or another were believed to be amenable to an anti-imperialist perspective.[93] Revolutionary forces in the Philippines were mindful of the connection between the United States' war in the Philippines and the treatment of blacks in the United States. A poster, printed in English and seized by United States forces, stated:

> To the coloured American soldiers: It is without honour nor profit that you are spilling your costly blood. Your masters have thrown you to the most inicuous [sic] fight with double purposes. In order to be you [sic] the instrument of their ambition. Your friends the Philipinos give you this good warning. You must consider your situation and your history. And take charge that the blood of your brothers Sam Heose and Gray proclaim vengeance.[94]

In other words, domestic politics could be harnessed and reframed to make compelling points about the United States' occupation of the Philippines.

Aspects of past domestic political issues also informed the thinking of anti-imperialist organizers. Steel magnate Andrew Carnegie suggested that the "dread of war" made investors nervous and served to stalemate economic growth.[95] German-American statesman, diplomat, abolitionist, and civil service reformer Carl Schurz relished being regarded as a crank, having "heard it so often—in connection with the anti-slavery movement, the civil service reform movement and other things—that I am rather used to it. It may be very fierce sometimes, but it always wears off if the cause provoking it is a good one."[96] Edward Atkinson, the long-time New England anchor to the Anti-Imperialist League's efforts, suggested that the nascent moral indignation of war atrocities in the Philippines would overcome "the spirit of greed, of war," even as people were not united on the course of action the United States ought to take in the islands, recalling that "we were not united against slavery but slavery went down."[97] United States Senator George Frisbie Hoar (R-MA), by contrast, believed that moral indignation over the United States' occupation of the Philippines was the same as that over slavery; whereas every defeat of abolitionists still did its part to weaken the institution of slavery, every defeat of anti-imperialists could not be counted as a victory. He noted that "if we get a government there in the hands of a set of ambitious and money-making officials and a system established there able to affect the Filipinos by patronage and jobs and corrupt methods, every year we shall be getting deeper and deeper into the mire."[98] In fact, Hoar suggested the strategy of "counting up to the American people their mistakes in the past," namely the United States' treatment of African Americans, Native Americans and Hawaiians.[99] Though their evaluations of the similarities and differences between these situations and that in the Philippines varied, past reform movements were the regular referents.

Whereas Charles Parkhurst questioned the wisdom of embarking on a colonial project in the Philippines when considering the condition of race relations in the United States, others argued against United States expansion by appealing to the turbulence of class relations. In *Republic or Empire? The Philippine Question* (1899), President of the American Federation of Labor Samuel Gompers contributed an essay that critiqued United States overseas expansion. Gompers questioned how Americans could reasonably expect its representatives in the Philippines to treat the islands' residents with due respect, when American workers were mercilessly murdered in the United States.[100] Others less prominent in national labor disputes also weighed in on the United States policy, finding that it would be detrimental to working people in the United States.[101] As historian Nell Irvin Painter has said of the Progressive Era, "The country was in crisis, threatened on one side by the evils of plutocracy—the myopic reactionaries whom President Taft represented—and on the other side by the mob."[102] If the abolitionist movement was the movement of the past, the burgeoning labor union movement was that of the present and dramatic change was afoot.

Charles Francis Adams had fought in the Civil War, and his experience in battle compelled him to lead a group of men to conduct an investigation of the alleged atrocities in the Philippines. Writing that he was "now expiating some of my own weaknesses and shortcomings of forty years ago," Adams figured that the strategy to "persistently thrust their own record into the Army's face" shamed them, and "That fact of shame,--the constant denial, the attempts at suppression, the brazen extenuations,--is the most hopeful feature in the situation. It forecasts improvement."[103] Adams's conviction that men would act when the shamefulness of their conduct was brought to light was itself animated by his experience in war and making amends for his own conduct during the Civil War.

As many Americans at the time would, Charles Francis Adams understood the Philippine-American War through the lens of the American Civil War—through which Adams not only lived, but also fought. Whereas he found the salvation of the United States in a "veil of oblivion" that covered the past of the Confederacy's secession, he found, too, the salvation of United States-Philippine relations in President Roosevelt's proclamation of amnesty and the war's end.[104]

While Adams believed that sending the memory of war into "oblivion" was an important phase in peace-making efforts, he also believed that eagerness to do so ought to be tempered by an honest recognition of what had happened in war.[105] There were at least two reasons for this, at once practical and ideological. The reconstruction of the Philippines under American rule could not be effectively administered without the recognition of the war's atrocities, necessary for understanding Filipinos' discontent. Second, the atrocities of the United States military needed to be recognized—for the maintenance of national character, to indicate that Americans' intentions were indeed benevolent. In fact, Adams's conviction that an American ought to be sent to the Philippines to investigate conditions was informed by his assessment of Reconstruction in the United States.[106]

When speaking before the Senate in opposition to the Organic Act in 1902, after revelations about the United States' military forces war atrocities in the Philippines had rocked the United States, Massachusetts Senator George Frisbie Hoar compared the wanton violence in the islands to acceptable violence in America. If the United States government had the right to begin a war and torture people of the Philippines, just as it had the right to do so "at home," then he had the same right to question the government's conduct: "I have the same right as an American citizen or an American Senator to discuss the conduct of any military officer in the Philippine Islands that I have to discuss the conduct of a marshall or a constable or a captain in Pittsburg or in Cleveland if there were a labor riot there."[107]

The violence of labor disputes in the United States, understood alongside war atrocities in the Philippines, of course, indicated the extent of Hoar's critique of draconian efforts to suppress social and political movements. Still in living memory were the economic depression of the 1870s and the attendant labor disputes of that decade, including strikes by Pennsylvania miners and railroad workers across the United States, that prompted state or federal intervention that turned violent. Such a politically volatile context provided a way for people in the United States to grasp what was happening in the Philippines. This way of framing the conditions in the islands—with reference to violence in the United States—would endure throughout the early years of the American occupation in the Philippines.

In this light, the United States' occupation of the Philippines was sometimes justified by its supporters in political or economic terms, and the protest to it was grounded in moral terms. Yet, the urgency and force of a moral argument depended upon the economic climate. Andrew Carnegie agreed, writing that "Our revenue are great and the masses are prosperous at present, therefore the huge expenditures of the government are not criticized. Wait till the wheel turns and we enter upon a period of depression, then every dollar taken will cause protest."[108] In any event, Charles Adams' analysis of the situation in 1903 serves as a reminder of the widespread labor disputes and lynching of African-Americans. Adams believed that economic prosperity could quiet critique of such violence in the United States, and that it could quiet critique of violence in the faraway Philippines.[109]

While Parkhurst, Gompers, Carnegie and others judged the American war in the Philippines harshly, with a regretful eye to the Civil War, writer and historian Charles Morris argued that, at the very least, the Spanish-American War had the fortuitous effects of both "removing the shreds of ill feeling remaining between North and South" and arousing "a strong sentiment of affinity between the Anglo-Saxon peoples of the earth."[110] If this was the case, the weight of the dispatches of American war correspondents in the Philippines and the speeches and writings of colonial officials amounted to an even more considerable body of work against which anti-imperialist arguments were posited. In the light that Morris cast, anti-imperialists were opposed to a war that reunited a divided nation.

The Anti-Imperialist League

Moorfield Storey, Edward Atkinson, Erving Winslow, and Charles Francis Adams all remained vocal critics of the United States' cause in the Philippines, and participated to varying degrees in the anti-imperialist movement throughout the beginning of the twentieth century. However, their approaches to organizing against United States policy in the Philippines differed in light of the official conclusion of the Philippine-American War. With the end of the conflict, the general American public received less news about the Philippines than it had previously, and while debate about colonial rule continued the coverage did not compare in sensationalism to the coverage of recent wars. Later efforts to pass the Jones Act were perhaps even less glamorous, with the details of the legislation failing to capture and hold the public's imagination.

After the passage of the Jones Act on August 29, 1916, the role of the Anti-Imperialist League was even less clear. Mandating the establishment of a Philippine Senate, the law was hailed by some as an important step in Philippine independence. In letters to Erving Winslow, Moorfield Storey expressed surprise at the league's influence and seemed to wonder if it should not fall quietly out of existence.[111] As World War I raged in Europe, participants in and supporters of the Anti-Imperialist League held varied opinions of how the organization ought to proceed. Some believed that the group ought to refrain from its usual outspoken critiques of the United States government, at least while "in the present of so much vaster matters and dangers and sacrifices."[112] In addition to echoing the view that the United States government had larger issues with which to deal, Moorfield Storey doubted the wisdom of further actions during the war on account of the possibility of the group "irritating the very persons whom we wish to conciliate" and the uncertainty of how further action of the Anti-Imperialist League would actually be of service to the Philippines at a moment of global upheaval.[113] Others suggested that the scope of the Anti-Imperialist League should broaden to address the United States' "imperialist doings" in other parts of the world.[114]

Unsurprisingly, conflicts were not limited to those between supporters of the United States' policy in the Philippines and "antis," and did not only arise after 1916. Within what was known as a rather monolithic anti-imperialist movement, conflicts arose. These conflicts appear to have as much to do with political strategy as personal differences. Very shortly after the formation of the Anti-Imperialist League, one of its most formidable and influential allies Senator George Frisbie Hoar of Massachusetts, wrote that several of the men involved with the anti-imperialist movement (Edward Atkinson, Charles Francis Adams, and Carl Schurz) had "been opposed to nearly everything the American people have believed in and have done for the last twenty years—however much they may be in the right now—and are not likely to lead a movement of this kind to success."[115] Lovering regarded Edward Atkinson as "just the man who in a storm would be likely to interfere with the helmsman."[116] Politically hostile to anti-imperialists, W. Cameron Forbes wrote in his journals

> Dougherty, the Chicago Anti-Imperialist is here, another wild-eyed fanatic who is, however, saner than Fiske Warren, but by no means sane. He came to see me one day and told me that Fiske had issued an Anti-Imperialist leaflet

calling for my resignation. I am rather proud of that. If he'd been satisfied with my work and character I should have begun to feel uneasy.[117]

James LeRoy, who worked as Dean Worcester's secretary but nevertheless counted himself among those "who do not believe in a colonial policy for our country," too, was critical of New England anti-imperialists.[118] George Frisbie Hoar conceded to fellow Massachusetts Senator Henry Cabot Lodge that "The cause of anti-imperialism, as it is termed, has been so managed that Bryan has made it odious to the West, and its managers in Boston have made it ridiculous in the East."[119]

Erving Winslow, one of the most visible and active leaders of the Anti-Imperialist League, managed to raise the rankle of not only his enemies but also his closest allies. Manuel Quezon explained to H. Parker Willis that "it is a pity that we should be handicapped by such a man who does not seem to have any conception of practical politics."[120] By 1919, Quezon had decided to stop corresponding with Winslow, as the latter challenged Quezon's and Osmeña's dedication to the cause of Philippine independence. Writing to Moorfield Storey, Quezon hoped that breaking with Winslow would not also damage his relationship with the Anti-Imperialist League.[121]

One of the critiques of the work of the Anti-Imperialist League, the entity central and most readily identified with the anti-imperialist movement in the United States, was its exclusive use of "genteel" approaches to agitating against the United States' policy in the Philippines.[122] Certainly one of the results of the Anti-Imperialist League's approach was the creation of an enormous body of material about the United States' involvement in the Philippines. Several active members of the Anti-Imperialist League were also prolific authors. In addition to these volumes, the Anti-Imperialist League—in New England and elsewhere—produced a variety of pamphlets and fliers that discussed and critiqued the United States' involvement in the Philippines. Beyond these publications, individuals in the Anti-Imperialist League also initiated and organized their own investigations. For example, H. Parker Willis traveled to the Philippines to report on conditions there, and private citizens examined evidence of war atrocities committed by Americans in the Philippines.

The creation of this body of work, at least in the organization's early years, was necessitated by what the leadership of the Anti-Imperialist League considered a dearth of reliable information about the Philippines in circulation. The scarcity of information about the Philippines for American audiences signaled different opportunities—military, academic, commercial—for different segments of the population. For the Anti-Imperialist League, the gap in the record of American actions in the Philippines marked a space that could be filled with information that reframed the dominant analysis of the United States' involvement in the islands and offered a corrective to the notion that the American presence in the Philippines was wholly benevolent.[123]

The leadership of the Anti-Imperialist League were not only concerned with the crisis in the Philippines. They were also invested in the project of creating an anti-imperialist archive. At an Executive Committee meeting of the New England Anti-Imperialist League, for example, it was "voted that the Secretary be authorized and requested to make a chronological record of the principal facts in the history of Anti-Imperialism and a bibliography of the movement, with a view to its future publication."[124] And when mention of the Anti-Imperialist League failed to appear in James Blount's *American Occupation of the Philippines, 1898-1912* in 1913, Erving Winslow complained to Manuel Quezon that the omission from Blount's "interesting and really quite monumental book" actually indicated "some sinister motive."[125] Likewise, as is most evident in the views of Charles Francis Adams, the anti-imperialist historian, the documentation and preservation of a viewpoint, however unpopular and unheeded at the moment, would maintain on the written record. According to Carl Schurz, Adams had "the peculiar strength as the representative of what is supposed to be the conservative element on the anti-imperialist side."[126] Of course, Charles Francis Adams was just one of several authors involved with the Anti-Imperialist League.

Edward Atkinson and *The Anti-Imperialist*

The experience of Anti-Imperialist League Vice-President Edward Atkinson highlights the varied and sometimes conflicting strategies of adherents to a broad anti-imperialist cause. At the same time, his work illustrates the ways that the United States' martial rule in the Philippines at once circumscribed and fueled the generation of an anti-imperialist archive.[127] In other words, though intended to contain the circulation of Edward Atkinson's *The Anti-Imperialist*, the actions of the United States government prompted even more discussion about and requests for access to Atkinson's work.

Under the rule of Governor-General Taft, the delivery of mail and other information into or out of the Philippines was the subject of considerable legislation. Censorship of the mail by the military authorities and the Director-General of Posts for the Philippine Islands was considered acceptable practice. This included the postcards that featured revolutionary leaders as they were considered "to be attempts to revive the memories of the Insurrection and to encourage the hope of another [...]."[128] Meanwhile, in the United States, journalists and others sympathetic with the anti-imperialist cause were critical of these censorship efforts. Libel and sedition laws discouraged and punished criticism of the new colonial administration, and the censorship of mails was designed to prevent criticism in the islands from reaching the United States. The lack of information arriving in the United States from the Philippines made balanced analysis of the situation difficult.[129]

According to his own account of events, Atkinson authored a series of pamphlets about the costs, financial and otherwise, of an American war in the Philippines with the intention of circulating them among "economic students and legislators."[130] Though he had requested from the Department of War a list of 500 or 600 names of military personnel to whom he could send his pamphlets, Atkinson had, in fact, only sent his pamphlets to Jacob Gould Schurman, Dean Worcester, J.F. Bass (a journalist with *Harper's Weekly*), Admiral George Dewey, General H.G. Otis, Henry Lawton, and one other individual with the last name Miller. The Postmaster General—whether mistakenly believing that the mailing of pamphlets were to be sent to several hundreds of people or not—ordered them removed from the mails and prevented from leaving San Francisco and going on to the Philippines. [131]

The debacle with the United States Postmaster General earned Atkinson some supporters.[132] At the same time, the widespread circulation of his views also provides glimpses into how unfavorably he was viewed. One recipient of Atkinson's pamphlet reported that he had destroyed it upon receipt, having "no sympathy with the publication or with the weak, traitorous minds that inspire it," and at least two public libraries refused to include the gift in their collections.[133]

On balance, however, the action of the United States government to stop the mailing of Atkinson's pamphlets in the United States—rather than, say, destroying them upon receipt in the Philippines—seems generally to have been understood as a misstep of, at the very least, the Postmaster General, and at the highest possible level, President McKinley. Atkinson was confident that his work had ignited "a spark to start the suppressed indignation all over the country."[134] Even Winslow Warren agreed that Atkinson's scheme may produce some good effect, noting the resonance between *The Anti-Imperialist* and abolitionist works: "My impression is that the same course was pursued as to "Uncle Tom's Cabin" and the "Liberator" and the results are sufficiently plain."[135] Thus by drawing attention to *The Anti-Imperialist* by stopping their mailing, the United States government created a situation where Atkinson and his work were actually garnering more attention than they might have otherwise.

Philippine Information Society and Jacob Gould Schurman

Of course, other individuals and organizations, not necessarily attached to the Anti-Imperialist League, also criticized the United States' policy in the Philippines. One organization was the Philippine Information Society. Founded in Boston, the Philippine Information Society published and circulated information about the United States' actions in the Philippines. The Society served as an alternative to the Anti-Imperialist League, the latter being known as relatively strident. Though it might seem that the Philippine Information Society would be a welcome party to the discussion on the United States' policy in the Philippines, with the two organizations together covering a broader political spectrum, the work of the Philippine Information Society garnered some private disdain from at least one individual closely involved with the work of the Anti-Imperialist League for precisely its more conservative orientation.[136] Thus, even as the Philippine Information Society and Anti-Imperialist League shared concerns about the United States' occupation of the Philippines and similar strategies to voice those concerns, their memberships did not necessarily work closely together.

Just as the Philippine Information Society was an organization at the center of some private criticism of other anti-imperialists, Jacob Gould Schurman was a prominent individual subject to criticism, and alternately praise, from people on both sides of the United States' policy in the Philippines. While President of Cornell University, Schurman had been appointed to chair the United States' first commission to the Philippines in 1899; this group—officially named the United States Philippine Commission and sometimes referred to as the Schurman Commission—was composed of Schurman, Military Governor of the Philippine Islands Elwell Otis, George Dewey, Charles Denby, and Dean Worcester. Its charge from President McKinley was to investigate conditions in the Philippines and make recommendations for the United States' course of action there. When the Philippine Commission submitted its report to President McKinley, Philippine nationalist aspirations for an independent Philippine Republic were dealt a setback, and Schurman earned the esteem of many McKinley supporters in the United States. Indeed, Schurman received a note from McKinley's secretary, reporting the President having been "very much pleased with what he has seen of your speech in Chicago," and throughout 1900, Schurman delivered several addresses on the Philippines, all of which were thought to be "doing great good."[137]

By early 1902, however, Schurman's views on the Philippines had changed—from a perspective that wholly supported the Republican policy in the islands to a perspective that questioned the wisdom of retaining the islands—and with this change of view came a change in Schurman's own supporters and detractors. After publishing *Philippine Affairs: A Retrospect and Outlook*, Schurman received a kindly letter from the publisher W.D. Howells, who noted that, "Your speech on the Philippine situation is full of a manly humanity. [...] You have struck the true note. If we are not in the Philippines to help their people to a safe independence, we are wrongfully there."[138] Schurman's swing to an anti-imperialist view was praised, and resulted in requests to write about the Philippines for *The Independent* and to participate as a member of the investigating committee that Charles Francis Adams hoped to convene.[139] By the spring of 1902, Schurman was even the recipient of conciliatory letters from Filipino nationalist Sixto Lopez:

> The policy which you advocate is, in my humble judgment, the one that will bring permanent peace and contentment not only to the Filipinos but to the heart and mind of every true American who desires to see the ideals and duties of the Republic maintained and performed.
>
> I do not wish to disguise the fact that I have differed from you in the past, perhaps through misapprehension of your motives and views, for I know how easy it is to misjudge an opponent, especially from a distance. But I trust that any mere flesh wound that have been inflected on either side in the contest for the right have long since healed.[140]

This warm sentiment of Lopez in 1902 had its correlate from the Taft administration. In fact, William Howard Taft's unkindly suspicion was that Schurman's real purpose in his participation in debates about the United States' policy in the Philippines was simply to "keep in the public eye."[141]

Schurman's presence "in the public eye" was noteworthy not only because as a president of a large university, he had wide visibility, but also because as head of the first Philippine Commission he had been one of few American government officials in the islands. His commission was the first to meet extensively with individuals to discuss the political and social conditions in the Philippines, and such experience earned Schurman political currency. In 1899, Stanford University President David Starr Jordan had observed that "We know nothing of Philippine matters, save through cablegrams passed through government censorship, and from the letters and speech of men of the army and navy. The letters and cablegrams do not always tell the same story."[142] Years later, Representative William A. Jones would echo Jordan's sentiment, though he would not go so far as to suggest the government's misdeed of censorship. Rather, he suggested that the administration in the United States relied on select, but not entirely dependable, sources that were bound to support American policy.[143]

H. Parker Willis and *Our Colonial Problem*

It was due to these concerns that members of the Anti-Imperialist League developed plans to send an American to the Philippines to gather, report, and publicize information about conditions in the islands. Charles Francis Adams, Jr., had headed a committee of men to investigate the allegations of war atrocities in the United States military's campaigns in the Philippines.[144] Over the course of this investigation, it became clear to Adams that the information coming out of the Philippines was not always reliable. Colonial officials had a vested interest in portraying the conditions in the Philippines in a positive light, and their reports reflected that interest. Newspaper correspondents were sometimes charged with the motivation of selling newspapers, returning servicemen were discredited as disgruntled or embittered, soldiers in the field could not write freely about conditions in the islands, for fear that some retribution may be taken, and, whether in the Philippines or the United States, unfavorable accounts were believed to be censored.[145] In other words, while all such information would provide an alternate assessment of the United States' course of action in the Philippines, there remained a compelling case for sending someone to the islands to conduct an investigation.

Adams, Schurz, and Welsh correctly anticipated that anyone sent to the Philippines from the United States to assess the conditions there in general, and the work of the occupation government in particular, was bound to meet some resistance. For this reason, they conducted their affairs with a degree of secrecy. Adams wrote to Schurz of the wisdom of "proceed[ing] very cautiously, putting as little in writing, outside of our own circle, as possible. I, of course, have to communicate with you and Mr. Welsh, frankly and frequently; but, so far as the public is concerned, it seems best to preserve a religious silence."[146] The work of creating an alternative archive sometimes required a concerted effort to not document work for the anti-imperialist cause.

Willis's preparation for the trip included reading available sources on the Philippines and obtaining letters of introduction (by his own account, upwards to 100) to colonial government workers. H. Parker Willis arrived in the Philippines in May 1904, by way of Hong Kong. Once in Manila, he regularly reported his findings back to the United States.[147] Willis spent the spring in Manila conducting interviews and writing up notes, and the summer traveling through several provinces—Rizal, Cavite, Batangas, Laguna, Bulacan, Bataan, Tarlac, Pangasinan, Mindoro, Romblon, Masbate, Cebu, Zamboanga, Jolo, Pampanga, and Morong—to conduct interviews there.

His method was, first, to read all of the official published reports on a particular topic, then conduct interviews with "unofficial persons in Manila (sometimes with subordinate government officials, who were discontented, or with local journalists, or with critical natives, or with army officers hostile to civil rule)." In synthesizing the information gathered in these interviews, Willis identified controversial points or policies about which he then interviewed "the higher official persons who were conversant with or responsible for the existing facts" with the hope of obtaining "categorical statements on the converted points." Willis concluded with site visits and interviews with local officials at those sites, before drafting his own analysis of a situation. He indicated that he employed a Filipino, Simeon Kison, for interviewing "with natives who were under surveillance and who could not safely receive visits from travelling Americans, as well as in obtaining information on topics outlined by me." In the provinces, Willis simply spoke directly with native officials and American school teachers. He left Manila in August 1904.[148]

Despite Willis's precautions, the purpose of his stay in the Philippines was soon known among Americans in Manila. After having been in the islands only about one month, Willis reported that the Philippine Commission was tracking his movements. Fortunately for his investigation, by that point, he had already gotten all the material that he wanted from other colonial officials. When it became impolitic for serving colonial officials to speak with Willis and difficult for him to gather information from interviews with this group, Willis turned to natives, soldiers, and ex-government employees.[149] In addition to interviews with various groups in the capital, Willis traveled to the southern islands in the archipelago, studied legislation of the Philippine Commission, establishment of public schools, administration of civil service, and government censorship of local media. Writing from the Philippines, many of Willis's reservations about and criticisms of the colonial administration were confirmed.[150]

The challenges that Willis faced while conducting his research in the Philippines continued upon his return to the United States. On top of personal attacks, Parker initially had trouble placing his work with a publisher.[151] Published by the Henry Holt Company in 1905, *Our Philippine Problem: A Study of American Colonial Policy* provided a detailed critique of nearly every aspect of the colonial administration, offered recommendations for how to improve the situation in the Philippines, and ultimately, advocated for "a declaration of the intention to work toward independence, and a distinct definition of the time when such independence may be possible." Moreover, Willis suggested, such a declaration would "render it easier, not harder, to govern the natives in the interim [...]."[152]

Charles Francis Adams's investment in the two investigations—first, the investigation that resulted in a report to President Roosevelt and, second, the investigation that resulted in H. Parker Willis's *Our Colonial Problem*—was complex and suggest some of the larger issues at work when people in the United States considered the actions of the government in the Philippines. From the beginning, he disapproved of the United States' course of action in the islands, but he was especially offended by revelations of torture executed by United States forces in the course of war. His efforts to coordinate investigations of the military's conduct was to put on record the actions of the government before proceeding with a colonial policy with which he continued to disagree. Though he understood that both government officials and the general public were "weary of the topic" and ready for "fresh fields and pastures new," he thought that a record of past misdeeds was important for moving forward. And once the record was made and acknowledged and perchance sent into oblivion, all parties could then proceed.[153]

As evidenced by H. Parker Willis' trip to the Philippines, the actions of the Anti-Imperialist League were not limited entirely to the United States. While the work of the Anti-Imperialist League was often the subject of ridicule in both the Philippines and the United States, the league's conviction that their efforts affected some change and discomforted the United States' colonial administrators was confirmed in at least one important instance. In 1901, for example, Boston lawyer Fiske Warren was reported to have traveled to the Philippines on the same boat as Sixto Lopez and other members of the revolutionary government to see if he, too, would be requested to take an oath of his acceptance of United States sovereignty in the islands.[154] Writing to Secretary of War Elihu Root about the legislative work of the Philippine Commission, Taft wrote that while a sedition law was not yet passed, the Commission sought to do so shortly. Taft noted that "We anticipated that that fool Fiske Warren of Boston, with Sixto Lopez may come here and that Lopez may feel called upon to say the things he has been permitted to say in America. If so, we shall prosecute him and we desire to have the law in such shape that the prosecution may be effective."[155] Even in the years after the conclusion of the Philippine-American War, when the importance and influence of the Anti-Imperialist League was widely supposed to be on the wane, officials in the United States and the Philippines sometimes found reason for concern. When an entertainment manager was reported to be neglecting a group of Filipinos, for example, Chief of Bureau of Insular Affairs Frank McIntyre wrote to Governor-General Henry Ide that if they were not provided passage back to the Philippines, the Anti-Imperialist League which was "hunting for grounds to make us trouble," would generate unwanted publicity for the United States administration in the Philippines.[156]

Even framing the writings of the leadership of the Anti-Imperialist League in this manner, the generation and circulation of monographs, pamphlets, and other materials may still be considered an outmoded and less effective way of having tried to organize an anti-imperialist movement. The publications of the Anti-Imperialist League somewhat lacked the sensationalism of muckraking journalists of the period. The Anti-Imperialist League's war of words was rather tame when considered alongside the protests of thousands, and sometimes tens of thousands, of workers in the streets of American cities. Still, we can understand the work of the Anti-Imperialist League alongside other archive-building projects at the end of the nineteenth century and beginning of the twentieth century, in that the league's efforts are in keeping with the model of creation, distribution, and preservation of records that enjoyed currency at the time. Consider the work of the Anti-Imperialist League alongside that of the Bureau of Insular Affair's *Philippine Insurgent Records* and imperialist sensibilities in general, and the prospect of creating an alternative archive is even more considerable and daunting.

Conclusion: The Martial Origins of Civilian Archives

> "We have here the history of the Filipino insurrection, written in official documents; not invented, not done with exaggeration but taken from the archives where the decrees and the dispositions of the general government are kept."
> --Javier Borres y Romero, 1897[157]

The forces against which the members of the Anti-Imperialist League and like-minded people struggled were formidable. The *Compilation of Philippine Insurgent Records*, the endless stream of "yellow" journalism, and *The Philippine Islands, 1493-1898* worked in tandem to create a case in support of the United States' course of action in the Philippines. The work of Captain John R.M. Taylor suggested the dangers of the native "insurgents", the popular press sang the praises of the United States military exploits in the islands and painted not a somber, but a glorious, picture of war; and the work of James Alexander Robertson and Emma Helen Blair provided the entire endeavor with a particular Spanish colonial frame, primarily academic in its pretensions. In short, these works provided military, popular, and scholarly cases for the military occupation of the Philippines. In later years, after the official conclusion of the Philippine-American War—even as coverage of the Philippines in national newspapers and magazines waned—the works of Taylor, Robertson and Blair would endure, when a reminder for the purpose and value of a civilian occupation, the establishment of a colonial government, was required.

Considering the moment in this manner—in terms of the generation and circulation of material that would serve contemporary political and commercial purposes, as well as endure for later ones—the approach of the Anti-Imperialist League deserves review. The rallies and public meetings that the Anti-Imperialist League hosted were undoubtedly tame events, compared with the marches and strikes by working people all over the United States. Yet, the work of the Anti-Imperialist League—to compile statistics and testimony, to draft polemics, and to circulate any and all information that ran counter to the glowing reports about war in the Philippines—may be understood in terms of building an archive that ran counter to that created by Taylor's division in the Department of War, Hearst's newspapers, or Robertson and Blair's edited volumes.

Indeed, while they may have been rightly critiqued by their contemporaries for being satisfied with "bearing witness" to the injustices committed by the United States, these testimonies nevertheless remain—opposed to the military and civilian occupation of the Philippines. The attention of the Anti-Imperialist League to an American tradition of exploitation of Native Americans and African-Americans on the continent, and the country's misdeeds in the Pacific and Caribbean, and their consistent framing of the situation in the Philippines with these events, were considered, by at least one ally, to be detrimental to the cause in the Philippines. However, it was undoubtedly in keeping with thinking historically about the United States. The attention of at least some of the Anti-Imperialist League's members to the league's place in the story of the late nineteenth and early twentieth century may be, ungenerously, considered among the members' inflated and unwarranted sense of their own importance. Still, when considered in terms of creating a viable and vying historical record, upon which later generations may rely, such attention seems a more sympathetic and reasonable approach.

As discussed in the previous chapter, the United States' military actions in the Philippines created a political need for what would become an enormous archive of material on the islands. More than simply a library of material, this body of work encompassed a broad variety of media, sought to include both old and current documents, and was supposed to be of future administrative and historical use. Whether the ceded Spanish documents or Taylor's English translations, these records spanned centuries of colonial and revolutionary life, all for the purpose of facilitating the United States' military occupation and later civil government of the Philippines. In short, war was the motor that drove the creation of the United States' first archives on the Philippines.

These resulting government archives compelled the creation of complementary and oppositional non-governmental archives. While some accounts of the United States' involvement in the Philippines were celebratory or otherwise supportive, a vocal minority also provided arguments for why the United States' course of action was not ideal. What was clear enough to members of this vocal minority was their sense that while the body of material the United States government was amassing on the Philippines was enormous, the public's access to that material was limited. That is, if war was the motor that drove the generation of a government archive on the Philippines, that resulting government archive was the motor that subsequently drove the generation of a non-governmental archive.

This examination of the archive amassed as a direct result of war in the Philippines—the cession of Spanish records, the translation of Filipino records, the publication of American records—suggests that archives of material relating to United States-Philippine relations at the end of the nineteenth century and beginning of the twentieth century have undeniably martial origins. These origins are important to keep in mind when beginning the project of understanding archives' relationship to matters of an apparently strictly civil nature, namely the disposition of land and the development of a colonial economy. The colonial bureaucracy's ability to obscure its own martial origins not only enabled the entrenchment of the United States' colonial state, but it enabled that state's representatives to boast of the government's efficiency in maintaining the colonial order. In short, obscuring the martial origins of civil order made room for colonial celebration where anti-colonial revolution had been.

CHAPTER 4
ARCHIVES AND LAND

> During generations the processes of empire have been working, unobserved in the United States. Through more than two centuries the American people have been busily laying the foundations and erecting the imperial structure. For the most part, they have been unconscious of the work that they were doing, as the dock laborer is ordinarily unconscious of his part in the mechanism of industry. Consciously or unconsciously, the American people have reared the imperial structure until it stands, to-day, imposing in its grandeur, upon the spot where many of the founders of the American government hoped to see a republic.
> --Scott Nearing, *The American Empire*[158]

Introduction

In the final decades of the nineteenth century and opening decades of the twentieth century, the rise of industrial manufacturing in the United States gave rise to critique of how such industry changed living and working conditions. Individuals from ordinarily opposing sides in labor-management relations found common cause in opposing the United States' course in the Philippines. Scott Nearing's analysis, however, differed from those offered by labor leader Samuel Gompers and industrialist Andrew Carnegie. Rather than invoking a notion of international solidarity or warning against empire's perils for national wealth, Nearing likened every American to "the dock laborer" insofar as both are unconscious of their work in constructing an "imperial structure" or a "the mechanism of industry." More an indictment than a lament, Nearing indicated that the United States' course might be changed once the unsavory, unconscious work for empire was presented to his readership.

While not referencing Frederick Jackson Turner explicitly, Nearing's 1921 discussion appears informed by Turner's 1892 discussion of the frontier in American history. Whereas Turner argued that territorial expansion was precisely American, Nearing argued that such expansion was not in keeping with American ideals. With twenty years, significant differences in political opinion, and the annexation of the Philippines, Puerto Rico, and Guam separating them, Turner and Nearing stood at opposing poles in the discussion of territorial expansion. Rather than settling the question of territorial expansion, however, the annexation and subsequent colonial rule of the Philippines raised the question again. In addition to envisioning a port that would facilitate trade with China and alleviate the problem of "overproduction," Americans saw the promise of the natural resources of the islands for commercial agriculture and mining, or more generally stated, saw the promise of the islands as a site for American investment capital. As fighting between United States and Philippine forces continued, of course, realizing the promise of the islands was impossible.

The Philippine-American War did not officially end until July 4, 1902, and hostilities continued for years afterward. Nevertheless, the United States inaugurated its Civil Government in the Philippines on July 1, 1901, and soon after, conflicts between the newly-installed civil occupation government and the entrenched military occupation government erupted. At the crux of the conflict between the military and civil government was a disagreement about how the islands' population would be most efficiently pacified, and which approach would lead to greater peace and prosperity. The three Military Governors in the Philippines between 1898 and 1901—Wesley Merritt, Elwell Otis, and Arthur MacArthur—had ruled with the belief that martial rule was the surest way to ensure safety in the islands, whereas Civil Governor Taft believed that civil rule would demonstrate the United States' benevolent intentions and thereby cultivate peace in the Philippines. Indeed, believing that continuing military rule would be "a fatal mistake," Taft wrote to Secretary of War Root that he believed that "the people are only waiting for an excuse to lose all insurgent sympathy or offishness, such as they now have, and to come in under the United States Civil Government."[159]

The territorial conflict between the Civil Governor and Military Governor, and later between the Governor-General and United States military forces in the Philippines was not simply metaphorical. Physical territory, too, was as central to the conflict between the military and civil government, as it was to the conflict between the United States and Philippine governments. During the first decades of American rule in the islands, land was allocated in one of a number of ways: military reservations, public lands, private lands, or friar lands. Military lands were allocated for use by American forces by the Philippine Commission; public lands were those lands ceded by Spain per the Treaty of Paris in 1898; private lands were those claimed by individuals or organizations with proper title; friar lands were those owned by the various religious orders. Matters of land ownership in the islands were considerably varied, and this variety proved meaningful, as the administration sought to cultivate the islands' economy, both in the sense of its capacity to generate income for the colony and in the sense of its capacity to generate that income with efficiency.

When appointed Governor-General, William Howard Taft, who had served previously as the first Civil Governor of the Philippines alongside Military Governors Otis (1898-1900) and MacArthur (1900-1901), had no higher authority in the islands to dispute his slogan and purported policy of "The Philippines for the Filipinos." The most literal, unqualified meaning of this slogan clearly did not stand, as in fact, the Philippines were for the Americans per the United States' Treaty of Paris with Spain. Still, the question of whom the islands should most benefit was insistent throughout the early years of the United States' colonial rule of the Philippines. How much more or less should the Philippines benefit than the United States? If the United States benefited more and the Philippines less, was it acceptable because the Philippines had benefited at all?

If the war-ravaged condition of the islands presented the United States with challenges to developing a profitable agricultural economy and entrenching a new colonial administration, it nevertheless offered room for some political maneuvering. The destruction of entire villages provided the United States with, on the one hand, the need and license for reconstruction as it saw fit, and on the other hand, a justified excuse for slow or stymied growth. The inauguration of major public works projects provides one example of this: Provincial roads were not nearly as extensive as they could have been under the Spanish regime, so the U.S. Philippine Commission's legislation for the construction of roads and bridges was an early and persistent priority, because public works were essential for the transport of goods. Likewise went the argument for improvements to the islands' ports and harbors. The opening of harbors to a greater degree than had been the case under the Spanish administration was thus understood to be an important piece of the execution of the United States' policy in the Philippines.

Economic prosperity would be measured through the extensiveness of the roads and bridges, the improvement of harbors, or the percentage of the total land of the islands recorded on title. The prerequisite for the administration's realization of such prosperity was the imposition of an American order, an ordering of land and labor. While such imposition was made difficult by the destruction of Spanish land records and the inadequacy of those still extant, the conditions did provide the United States with a compelling reason to impose a new Land Registration Act and build an archive of land records with, literally, the United States' colonial government's stamp on every document.

While such total order was determined to be required of the land, it was not achieved. Still, efforts to maintain archives and records provide a different way to see how these disruptions in the execution of United States policy to exploit Philippine natural resources came to pass. Bearing in mind Nearing's observation that everyday work builds the machinery of industry and empire, this chapter considers how archives and recordkeeping were integral to the colonial administration's economic development of the islands. More precisely, it examines the registration of land titles, the disposition of public lands, the paper trail of the friar lands controversy, and the branding of *carabao*, that archetypal beast of burden in the Philippines. These practices set the stage for the new—purportedly modern and efficient—United States bureaucracy that displaced the Spanish one.

Philippine Commission Land Laws

> "Before concluding it will not be too much to say that he who successfully regulates the adjustment of titles to the lands in these islands will merit a crown of glory, receive the congratulations of an obedient and grateful people, and guarantee the political policy which may be implanted, promote agriculture—the basis of wealth in any country—and prevent a possibility of a repetition of the evils of the past."
>
> --Forestry Bureau of the Philippine Islands, 1901[160]

The colonial administration needed an orderly and efficient system for maintaining land records to develop the colonial economy. The myriad complications associated with establishing such a system is evident in the notion that doing so would "merit a crown of glory." These complications included the destruction of land records throughout the revolution, the new colonial government administrators' finding fault in the surviving Spanish land records, and the expectations of American would-be settlers and investors, as well as their detractors. Resolving questions of title to privately-owned land, disposing of public lands by lease, sale, homestead, or ancestral claim, and settling the question of who could purchase the so-called friar estates—all of these tasks required either the consultation of existing archives of land records or the generation of new land records, and oftentimes benefited from both.

While not knowing the extent of the lands ceded from Spain to the United States per the Treaty of Paris was an important factor in planning for land disposition, another important aspect of the trouble was the domestic situation in the United States. The Philippine Bill, which allowed for the establishment of a civil government in the islands, showed the marks of negotiation that took into account public sentiment in the United States. Characterizing the land laws in the Philippines as "colored with excessive caution," Jose S. Reyes wrote that "Such solicitude for the public lands, for the friar lands, for the mines, the forests, the franchises, and the public debts arose more out of conditions in American history and politics than from an objective examination of Philippine needs and problems."[161] And, indeed, one strain of criticism of the colonial administration's sale of lands to Americans was informed by an awareness of the United States' dealings with American Indians.[162] Restrictions on the amount of public land that individuals and corporations could purchase were the result of the combined forces of those individuals loathe to see American exploitation of Philippine Islands land and the various trusts, specifically that of sugar, which stood to lose business should the Philippines be left wide open to foreign investors.[163]

Bureau of Public Lands

> "People have asked why the ownership of real estate should not be as readily ascertained, and transferred as easily, as the ownership of stocks and bonds; they have asked, and with reason, if there was anything inherent to land which debarred it from taking its place in the march of progress and ridding itself of the old and outgrown forms and practices fastened upon it in some epoch remote and different from our own."
> --Associate Judge D.R. Williams, Court of Land Registration, 1903[164]

It was in this political context that the Bureau of Public Lands was established with Act No. 218 of the Philippine Commission on September 2, 1901. Organized within the Department of the Interior, the Bureau had charge of much of the government-owned lands. The act required that the chief of the bureau collect and maintain Spanish land records, devise a plan to organize the bureau informed by land laws in the Philippines under the Spanish regime and in the United States, organize and oversee the surveying of lands, and report on the extent and quality of government-owned lands. Every one of the duties assigned to the bureau chief indicate how little the new colonial government knew about its acquired territory: the land records contained in the Spanish colonial state's archives were not centralized, and the colonial administration anticipated that as the Spanish records were collected, they would be found to be unsatisfactory. By creating a system for organizing records, the new Bureau of Public Lands laid the groundwork for the colonial government to suggest the necessity of its continued existence and increasingly broad powers.

While the charges of the Chief of the Bureau of Lands indicate the colonial government's intention of refashioning the system that the Spanish colonial government already had in place, and that such a refashioning would require a good deal of effort, the chief's various responsibilities also suggested that the Spanish system offered an object lesson in misadministration. Though the bureau chief was required to maintain the Spanish records and formulate a plan for the bureau's organization with the former land system in mind, the bureau was nevertheless to be "framed as nearly after the organization of the Public Land Office in the United States" as would be allowed. Assignment of titles to land facilitated re-settlement of Filipinos away from their ancestral lands. This re-settlement, in turn, provided the means and presumed mandate to establish postal and agricultural savings banks, the establishment of these institutions, and, more generally, the inculcation of a sensibility about land settlement were lessons in political education under the Americans.

In the same year that the Bureau of Public Lands was organized, Governor-General Wright signed Executive Order 93 (June 2, 1902) to authorize the bureau chief to certify documents therein relating to title, just as would a notary or other official authorized to certify documents. The order indicated an effort to streamline the generation and processing of records, in light of the volume of documents to come. Indeed, the legislation to organize the bureau and the executive order to expand the responsibilities of the bureau chief anticipated the work that would result from the passage of the Act 496, also known as the Land Registration Act. Passed by the Philippine Commission on November 6, 1902, the Land Registration Act enabled greater legislative and executive attention to be trained on building up an archive of land records to replace that ceded from Spain.

In the first year after the passage of the Land Registration Act, conditions in the islands required the law's amendment. With the civil colonial government more firmly established, the Philippine Commission passed Act 627 on February 9, 1903, which brought more land under the operation of the Land Registration Act, namely lands within military reservations, as well as lands that the United States wanted to purchase for military purposes. On March 26, the Land Registration Act was further amended, this time to detail the responsibilities of the Court of Land Registration and to provide for new forms for the Bureau of Public Land's "Certificate of Acknowledgment" and "Form of Acknowledgement," which were provided by the bureau to individuals seeking to register land. Further, this law mandated gathering of more information about such individuals, requiring the marital status of anyone applying for a grant, mortgage, or lease. These amendments reflected the incorporation of elements of the United States' martial rule into the everyday workflow of newly-organized civilian entities, as well as the normalization of gathering information about governed individuals. In short, they exemplify what Reynaldo Ileto has called "Knowing America's Colony," by means of creating a record of civil government lands.[165]

Publications in the *Official Gazette* originating from the Bureau of Public Lands and the Court of Land Registration suggest that the imposition of the Land Registration Act faced challenges in raising participation.[166] Two articles published in 1903 addressed questions of how and why people in the islands ought to apply to the state for access to lands. "Rules and regulations of the Court of Land Registration of the Philippine Islands" provided a concise listing of the required elements to registering land title with the colonial government. It offered a more easily digested report of information than did the lengthy law itself, intended for a broader readership.[167] The earlier of the two publications, an essay by an Associate Judge in the Court of Land Registration, "Operation of 'Land Registration Act'" explained that the law was "an attempt to apply to dealings with real property the same rules which are now applied by business men the world over in their dealings with personal property."[168]

The new system established the colonial office as the official center for all titles. If not registered with the bureau, the title was not legally recognized, nor were alterations to the title. This did not discount ownership per se, but in the event that a dispute about ownership arose the bureau would serve as the arbiter. In short, title ownership and transfer thereof began and ended with the new state. This system of land registration was established to alleviate doubts surrounding ownership of lands, which theretofore had made the negotiation of mortgages challenging and otherwise discouraged "the purchase and sale of real estate, thus preventing that free movement of property so essential to the progress and prosperity of a country."[169]

The Philippine Commission's efforts to develop a colonial economy continued with the passage of Act 926, also known as the Public Land Act, on October 7, 1903. This law outlined the different methods of acquiring public land, which required documentation of the same kind demanded by the Land Registration Act and, also contributed to the building up of a central depository of land records to replace the old, Spanish system. Shortly after the passage of the Land Registration Act, the Philippine Commission passed Act 1128 to differentiate the process of acquiring public lands containing coal and other public lands.[170]

These laws set the stage for the Bureau of Archives to become involved in the business of settling land titles. Governor-General Wright's Executive Order 41 (October 17, 1904) designated the Chief of the Bureau of Archives as "the custodian of all title deeds, leases, contracts of sale or purchase, and other documents of title appertaining to unassigned Insular Government lands and buildings throughout the Archipelago, including the City of Manila, unless provided by law in specific instances." Further, the Chief of the Bureau of Archives was required to "furnish to the Chief of the Bureau of Public Lands certified copies of such of said documents as the latter may from time to time request." For his part, the chief of the Bureau of Lands was obliged to provide to anyone interested in applying for title per the Public Land Act official blank forms—free of charge, in Spanish or English.[171]

With the change of the Bureau of Archives to the Bureau of Archives, Patents, Copyrights and Trademarks in 1905, the Bureau of Lands worked with that office to register, survey, and administer the islands.[172] While its work drew from the previous work of the United States to manage its other territories, the bureau still faced numerous problems—both internally and in its interactions with Filipinos.[173] In 1906, Governor-General Ide issued Executive Order 31 to address the issue of people being unable to correctly fill out the official blank forms for title to land, mandating that municipal secretaries must prepare applications without charge for individuals seeking land within such secretaries' municipalities.[174] As the scope of the colonial government expanded, bureaucrats in the colonial state not only provided such services to the public. They also supplied information from the amassed land records to facilitate other colonial projects.[175] The purpose of and challenges to the Bureau of Lands, when considered in tandem with the transactions that resulted in its records, illustrate the role that archives—the destroyed, the outdated Spanish, the new and modern American—were poised to play in remaking the Philippines into a land of homesteads and agricultural corporations.

While the purpose of imposing a new order on land through their survey and registration was to encourage small-scale agriculture among the Filipinos through settlement of uninhabited lands, the imposition also created a context in which colonial administrators could readily envision the Philippines in familiar terms of progress. Writing about his trip from Nueva Vizcaya to Isabela, Governor-General Forbes wrote:

> We passed through most lovely country all the way, great rolling slopes of hills, mostly bare, and covered with waving grass and occasional bits of woodland that remind you of northern New York and the Geneseo valley, a paradise; and finally Isabela, a vast level plain, the cruel part of it all being that it's wholly uncultivated. Here are thousands of square miles of country as lovely as any I ever saw, ranging from 2500 to 1000 or less, feet above the sea, and not a soul nor a domestic animal in sight.[176]

Forbes' observation that the Philippine landscape might remind someone of northern New York and the Geneseo Valley captures both his vision of promise and his unsympathetic view of many Filipinos' aversion to leave their homes to settle in other parts of the archipelago. Such aversion disrupted the former Secretary of Commerce and Police's plans for the development of unfarmed lands in the islands. Despite his political efforts, the "cruelty" of uncultivated land continued throughout Forbes' administration, and the development of agriculture—large- and small-scale—faltered.

Indeed, the lack of interest in resettling elsewhere continued beyond Forbes' tenure as Governor-General. The Philippine Legislature passed an act that extended the offer of free patents to Filipino settlers beyond the date determined in the Public Land Act, through the end of 1922.[177] In this instance—of building up the core of the colonial archive with the newly registered land titles under the United States' regime—failure was at least in part due to mistaken assumptions and expectations about how people in the islands would respond to new laws. As the duties of the Chief of the Bureau of Public Lands and Forbes' push for resettlement to other regions of the Philippines make clear, plans for the disposition and registration of land and the development of agriculture in the islands in the first decade of the twentieth century were modeled on the homesteading of public lands in the western territories of the United States. The mistaken expectation was that the colonial government's efforts on this front would yield results in the Philippines similar to those in the United States.

Friar Lands

> It is impossible to give chapter and verse in underhand dealings of which the records, if they exist, can only be got at under another Administration.
> --Erving Winslow[178]

In 1900, the records of "underhand dealings" to which Erving Winslow referred pertained to the deal brokered between the United States and the religious orders with land interests in the islands. When the United States acquired the Philippines from Spain per the Treaty of Paris, the United States acquired the public lands, also known as Crown lands. The United States did not and could not make claim to lands owned by private individuals or corporations, including the lands owned by the religious orders. The latter, commonly referred to as the "friar lands" presented a multi-faceted problem for the United States: Spanish friars were well known to abuse their power in the islands, and when the Philippine Revolution of 1896 broke out, many of these friars left the church estates for fear of punishment or death at the hands of Filipino revolutionaries. With acceptance of the treaty of peace between the United States and Spain, the question of what would happen to the friars remained. It was a disservice to all parties, it seemed, to allow the friars to return to the estates—Spanish friars had reason to fear for their safety, Filipinos had reason to loathe their return, and Americans would appear to condone their abuses if they allowed them to.

The solution that Civil Governor William Howard Taft brokered with the Vatican was the purchase of the friar lands and the provision for the friars' departure from the Philippines. This occurred over the course of two years and resulted in the purchase of the friar lands in 1904. When the agreed-upon price for the friar lands was eventually made public, some thought that it exceeded their market value. Others argued that the political peace enabled by the purchase was worth any monetary price. In the end, the United States Congress agreed to loan the money required for the purchase of the friar lands to the colonial government in the Philippines.

Thus indebted, the government of the Philippines was under obligation—how pressing an obligation is debatable—to aggressively sell lands, the profit from which would help to repay the loan from the government of the United States. Writing to Governor-General Smith in 1908, Bureau of Insular Affairs Chief Clarence Edwards saw a discrepancy between his view of the status of Friar estates and those maintained in the Philippines, noting that

> when Worcester was here he expressed confidence in the way [Bureau of Lands Chief] Captain Sleeper was taking hold, and everybody knows what a good reputation he has for executive ability, but after looking over these figures and trying to analyze them, I concluded that I am from Missouri, and I can't see where he, or anybody else, can gain any comfort out of such analysis, or for the future.[179]

Less than two years later as the controversy about the friar lands was beginning to stir, Edwards wrote to Smith's successor, Governor-General Forbes expressing the same reservations about the handling of the lands in the Philippines; he observed that the Philippine Commission's recommendation that corporations be permitted to purchase land at 6,000 hectares at a time could not come at "a more inopportune moment," as the trend toward the conservation of natural resources in the United States gained currency.[180] Edwards' successor, Frank McIntyre, wrote to Governor-General Gilbert that to facilitate the sale of the friar lands, the Philippine Commission should see to it that a law "making the price more elastic."[181] Such expressions of doubt and concern account for what would be later characterized by defenders of the colonial administration as pressure to expeditiously repay the debt incurred by the colonial state to purchase the friar lands.

Indeed, the means of easing this debt—namely, selling the friar lands—caused controversy. More specifically, the controversy surrounded three sales: the alleged proposed purchase of 55,000 acres by the Mindoro Development Company which was suspected of being connected with the "Sugar Trust" of the United Sates, the purchase of lands by a relative of the Secretary of the Interior Dean C. Worcester, and the purchase of lands by Executive Secretary Frank W. Carpenter. The controversy turned on whether the extent of public lands allowed for purchase by individuals and corporations per Act No. 496, more commonly known as the Land Registration Act, applied to the purchase of friar lands.

Of course, views of the propriety of these purchases varied, as did interpretations of the meanings of large land purchases by Americans. Chief of the Bureau of Insular Affairs Frank McIntyre wrote to former Philippine Commission David Barrows that he saw no problem with the actions—he thought that the controversy surrounding Carpenter was really a problem of perception, while he was surprised by Worcester's lack of supporters and defenders.[182] The Anti-Imperialist League determined to send a letter of protest to President Taft regarding the sale of friar lands, noting that such sales "tend to postpone the independence of the Philippine Islands and to embarrass the relations between the islands and the United States by creating interests adverse to the interests of the Filipino people."[183] The Resident Commissioners in the United States, Manuel Quezon and Sergio Osmeña, did not object to the sale of friar lands to individuals up to 40 acres per person, but Quezon did understand that the questions raised by the scandal had significant bearing on the people of the Philippines.

For Manuel Quezon, the question of the friar land estates raised "the question of the illegality of permitting Americans to purchase lands in the Philippines, a thing the Philippine Government has been allowing for years and years and nobody has paid any attention to it, nor found any fault with it," as well as the purpose of the United States having acquired the friar lands in the first place.[184] In Quezon's estimation, the purpose of the acquisition—"to sell these lands to their tenants on easy terms, even at a loss to the Philippine Government, in order to settle an agrarian question and a system of "absentee landlordism"—was woefully unrealized when "tenants on all these friar estates are discontented and assert that they are treated worse by the Government than they were by the friars."[185]

In 1910, a congressional committee was appointed to investigate the actions of the colonial administration, and the majority of the committee found the three accused parties to be not guilty of any wrongdoing, either in the letter or spirit of the public land laws. The committee ultimately submitted four reports. Of the three minority reports, one was signed by five members, a second by three members, and the final by a single member. The majority committee, with nine members signing, reasoned that the public lands laws applied only to lands that had been transferred from Spain to the United States. They did not apply to the friar lands, which were purchased through dealings between the Vatican and the Philippine government, not the United States government. Not only were the accused cleared of charges of wrongdoing, they were, according to the majority report, to be commended for taking seriously the financial obligations of the colonial government to the United States Congress and doing all in their power to sell the friar lands profitably. Looking back on the inquiry congressional inquiry, Quezon wrote to Representative Martin (D-Colorado), who had led the investigation, that even in light of the administrators' exoneration, some good had been achieved. Had attention not been drawn to the actions of colonial administrators, and the questions of ownership and purpose broached, "It would, in the long run, have deprived the Filipinos of their resources, and place them forever in political bondage."[186]

The friar lands scandal highlights two of the archival issues that were central to the colonial government's administration of lands. The first of these was the importance of differentiation of types of land as public, private, or friar. This differentiation depended upon reliable recordkeeping under the Spanish regime, and the proper transfer of such records to the United States upon its occupation of the islands. Second, the investigation of the colonial government's dealings required examination of the current condition of records in the Philippines. For those accused of wrongdoing, they would have been better situated had the hearings and investigations been held in the Philippines, since the vast majority of records were held there, such as they were. As it turned out, however, the hearings were held in Washington, D.C., requiring Governor-General Forbes, Secretary of the Interior Worcester, and Executive Secretary Carpenter to select materials and deliver them to the investigating committee. Worcester bitterly estimated that "some 8 tons of records" were transported from the Philippines to the United States for the hearings.[187] The requirements of this investigation occasioned an assessment of the condition of records in the Philippines, whether ceded from the former Spanish colonial government or created by the current American colonial government.

The sections of the Treaty of Paris appertaining to the transfer or reproduction of colonial records indicate that the United States and Spanish governments anticipated that these questions would arise. The Land Registration Act and the Public Lands Act, coupled with the shared workflow of the Bureau of Lands and the Bureau of Archives, underscored the absence of records or the inadequacy of existing records. Underlying all aspects of the disposition of land—whether private, public, or formerly owned by religious orders—were the economic questions of how the land of the Philippines could be used most profitably for United States interests, who should be permitted to use the land, and who should be able to determine these matters. The establishment of the Bureau of Lands in 1903, and its eventual cooperation with the Bureau of Archives, Patents, Copyrights, and Trademarks, answered these questions in part.

Public Lands

> "The organization of these offices [Mining and Forestry] as well as others which have followed, under legislation of the Philippine Commission, took on a bureaucratic character, and thus from the beginning Philippine administration in American hands was unified, centralized, and made responsible to the chief executive of the archipelago."
>
> --David P. Barrows, 1917[188]

In 1902, the Philippine Commission sent David P. Barrows to the United States for a month to investigate "the operation of Indian legislation and the organization of scientific work by the government," paying special attention to "irrigation on reservations, land allotment, Indian police, and Indian education."[189] The supposition driving Barrows' research was that the United States' dealings with American Indians would offer lessons for the new administration in the Philippines. By 1917 when Barrows published *The Pacific Ocean in History*, the former Philippine Commissioner could assess the organizational structure of the colonial administration. Though in this instance, the praiseworthy offices were the Bureau of Mining and the Bureau of Forestry, the ideal of central bureaucratic units accountable to the highest colonial officer in the Philippines, was one to which the directors of the other bureaus, including the Bureau of Archives and the Bureau of Lands, aspired.

Given the relationship between the Bureau of Archives and the Bureau of Lands appertaining to the gathering or generation, filing, storage, and retrieval of land records, however, centralization had to be split between the two units. Though all of the departments of the colonial government transferred their "dead" records to the Bureau of Archives, the relationship between the Bureau of Lands and the Bureau of Archives was more involved because the latter maintained the inactive and active records of the Bureau of Lands. Whether documentation of routine transactions of the colonial government units or registered land titles, the volume of records destined for the archives promised to be considerable. Even so, the creation of records associated with the disposition of public lands (titles, announcements, surveys) and the labor involved (research of Spanish archives, drafting of American titles, surveying of Philippine land) may have been the most ambitious, beginning early and ranging broadly.

The Land Registration Act, passed in 1902, set into motion the enormous project of attaching titles to lands throughout the islands. The Land Registration Act outlined the different ways that Philippine citizens, United States citizens, and citizens of other United States territories could acquire land in the Philippines—by demonstrating their continuous occupation of a parcel of land, by identifying land on which to homestead, by lease, by perfecting titles, grants or concessions obtained under Spanish sovereignty, or by purchase. The application process for making claim to land varied, but taken together, they all served to map the islands as a place of potential agricultural development. The voluminous records that constituted the application process also constituted an archive of land records that displaced the system operated under the Spanish regime. Even so, Filipinos were not eager to apply for titles to land by any of the means outlined by the Americans. In the first few years after the passage of the Land Registration Act, turnout was low, and the colonial government needed to identify ways to promote their project.

The result was a primer, published by the Bureau of Lands in 1906, that answered common questions relating to the acquisition of land. In addition to answering questions about which land was covered by the Public Land Law and how to obtain a free patent to public land, the primer also provided some explanatory context for why the public land law was in place. The primer explained that the reason there was so little private land in the islands was "Because the Filipinos have not tried hard to get land of their own. They have worked on the lands of other people. They have not often enough sought and planted new land for themselves." Explaining why Filipinos did not "try to get land for themselves," the primer offered

> They did not know where the public land was. They did not know how to get it. Also they did not like to move away from their homes to distant places. If a man wishes to have land and a home of his own, he must be willing to leave for a while his town and his amusements and friends. This is the way the early settlers of America and many other countries did.[190]

In short, the primer's ultimately faulty reasoning was that with some explanation of the project and the process, Filipinos would be eager to acquire title to land. The problem, supposed the bureaucrats at the Bureau of Lands, was a lack of information. While they were wrong in their identification of the problem, the resulting primer nevertheless provides a glimpse into why and how the colonial government sought to administer the disposition of lands and thus create a body of land records.

Current Occupants Claiming Title

> "Suppose the public land I wish is already occupied by someone. If the person living on the land is a person who has a right to gain a homestead or a free patent, he must be told his rights and given one hundred and twenty days to ask for the land. He has first claim during that one hundred and twenty days. If he does not ask the Government for the land he must leave the land. If he does not leave it you may ask the Director of Lands to compel him to leave."[191]

A person seeking to settle on public land had to determine that the land was public and available, by researching old Spanish land records, consulting longtime residents of the area, and determining the history of tax payments on the desired land. Of course, this route for acquiring public land was active, beginning with an individual who sought land and thus set into motion a series of inquiries into the records of the Spanish colonial regime that were held at the provincial level or centrally at the Bureau of Lands or the Bureau of Archives. The Bureau of Land's *Primer Containing Questions and Answers on the Public Land Laws in Force in the Philippine Islands* suggests something different. The hypothetical question here—of how to deal with public land already occupied—illustrates how engagement with the colonial government could be reactive. Research into the existing land records created under the Spanish regime and the generation of new land records under the American regime could very likely be the resulting effort of someone who simply desired not to be evicted from the land.

This American system for simultaneously accommodating settlers and documenting the expansive arable land of the archipelago was severe, and it found its antecedent in the Spanish colonial government's land laws. An unsigned report submitted to William Howard Taft in 1901 indicates how Spanish public land law would inform those to be imposed by the American colonial government in the Philippines. Under the Spanish system, most public lands were available for purchase—after notice and advertisement—by residents of the islands. There was no limit on the amount of land that could be bought, but it could not be had on credit and was awarded to the highest bidder. In instances where people were already living on land eligible for sale, proof of cultivation of or continuance residence on the land qualified them for titles before others.[192]

As it turned out, the Public Land Law, enacted October 7, 1903, nearly a century after the Spanish land law was passed, reflected the United States colonial administration's attention to the land laws of the previous regime. Under the Public Land Law, Filipinos were eligible to receive "free patents" for lands on which they lived, if they met certain criteria. These criteria were not identical to the Spanish land laws of 1804, but were similar in principle insofar as they limited the persons who could acquire land in the Philippines.[193] The challenge lay in providing sufficient proof of continuous occupation and cultivation, but given the eagerness of colonial administrators for Filipinos to register land title, the application process was less onerous than one may expect.

If an applicant met these criteria, he could then provide a written application to the provincial treasurer who also served as the local land officer. The application required statement of name, age, address, and whether the applicant was a native of the Philippines. It also required the name of the province he occupied, a description of the land, a statement that no one else already occupied the land, a statement of how long the applicant or his ancestors had lived on the land, and a statement of any improvements made to the land. "If the claim is based on the holding of land by an ancestor, the name of the ancestor and satisfactory evidence of the date and place of his death and burial must be given."[194] By so doing, the applicant provided the colonial government with a description of himself as well as the land it had annexed from Spain.

How this system would ideally work for the generation of land records is clear: a man would come upon land he cared to own. If another man already lived there, he would be told of the first man's desire to live on the land, and if he wanted to continue to live where he was, would apply to the Bureau of Lands for the right to homestead or for a free patent. If he chose not to apply to the Bureau of Lands, he would have approximately four months to arrange to leave the land. At that point, the first man could come and live upon the land and cultivate it. Regardless of who ended up living on and holding title to the land, that parcel would be accounted for in the land records.

Homesteads

> *"Why does the Government give homesteads to people?* Because it is better for the people to have land and homes of their own than to work for other people and live on the lands of others. People who have their own homes are better citizens and more prosperous than those who do not."[195]

Under the homesteads section of the Public Land Law, citizens of the Philippines, United States, or any of the United States' insular possessions were entitled to a homestead. The widespread settlement of Americans in the Philippines, however, was considered unlikely. At most, discharged American military men, Americans in the colonial civil service, and their families were anticipated to live for extended periods in the islands. Still, the land grab in the western territories of the United States offered a model for some Americans in the islands.[196] For these people, the prospect of homesteading or purchasing lands in the archipelago had some appeal.

Indeed, the war between Americans and Filipinos had hardly begun when the Bureau of Insular Affairs began fielding questions from Americans about the homesteading and investment prospects in the islands. Individuals inquired about what kinds of crops were suitable for the climate, how much land private individuals and companies could acquire, what support the United States government would provide for prospective American homesteaders, and whether the United States would honor Spanish concessions.[197] If some Americans thought they might make their name and fortune through service in the colonial government, others considered, with colonial government subsidies, finding their way through private enterprise.

The trouble that the colonial government faced in selling or homesteading public lands was more than enticing Americans from the United States or recently relieved United States soldiers. The colonial government was unsure which lands could be made available.[198]

Without a reliable survey of public lands at their disposal, the best that representatives of the colonial government could offer was directions to people who *might* be able to determine ownership. While such an assessment of the colonial government's handle on the status of ownership of lands caused some embarrassment to an administration eager to make economic inroads, the condition of the records—or more accurately, the absence of them—precipitated an ambitious cadastral survey under the Forbes administration as well as special reports of investigations into existing records from the chief of the Bureau of Archives.[199]

To obtain a patent to unoccupied public land per the homestead sections of the Public Land Law, applicants followed a course similar to that of applicants for free patents for land they or their ancestors had occupied. First, a prospective homesteader identified the land he wished to own and checked with the provincial treasurer/land officer who, in turn, determined whether the identified land was public or not, "as far as his records show." The prospective homesteader then completed and returned to the land officer a "Homestead Application, B.L. Form No. 7," after which the applicant was then required to have the form notarized and returned to the provincial treasurer/land officer with the application fee of ten pesos. Having turned in the form, the applicant then returned to the land and cultivated it. After five years, the applicant needed two men who would swear to his having lived on the land for five years, then send this "final proof" to the Bureau of Lands, along with another fee of ten pesos. Upon receipt of this final payment, the status of the land was recognized and official.[200] Thus, these records passed through many hands—statements from the applicant, notarization from a certified notary, review by the provincial treasurer, transmittal to the Bureau of Lands in Manila, and finally the issuance of a patent to the applicant. Through this process, the extant Spanish land records were complemented and perfected, resulting in American land records that conformed to the requirements outlined by the new regime's land laws. As in the case of current occupants making claims on lands, the application process for homesteads served the twofold purposes of providing information on individuals and on land.

Lease and Purchase

The Public Land Law instituted a similar application process for the leasing of public lands. The prospective lessee had to submit to the provincial treasurer/land officer an application with his name, address, and citizenship, as well as a statement that the land did not contain valuable minerals or timber and was more valuable for agricultural purposes than all others. In addition, however, people or corporations who intended to lease public lands had to make public notice of their intention in no less than in six places, thus inviting more attention than did the application process for free patents or homesteads.[201]

A number of forces appear to have been at work in the crafting of regulations on the lease or purchase of lands. While the homesteading section of the land law provided the means by which private individuals could purchase land, this section of the land law provided the means by which groups of individuals or corporations could purchase land. The most important aspect of the law was the restriction on the number of hectares that a corporation could purchase. The law provided that corporations could own no more than 2,500 acres for commercial agriculture. The law provided one loophole for corporations, however, as there were no limits on the amount of land that could be acquired for the irrigation of lands purchased for commercial agriculture.

Unperfected Titles and Spanish Grants and Concessions

The colonial government also had to deal with instances where individuals claimed title to land but had no proof that they had acquired it from the Spanish colonial government previous to the arrival of the United States in the Philippines. For the most part, the procedure for individuals claiming to have had title to land under Spanish rule was similar as that for individuals looking to purchase, lease, or settle land, or make claim to land by their own or ancestral occupation.

The exception was that the former could make their claims through either the provincial treasurer/land officer or the Court of Land Registration rather than through the provincial treasurer/land officer per se. The reasons provided for why individuals would have to confirm their claim to land through the United States colonial government were that "the Attorney-General of the Philippine Islands has held that no title can be acquired against the Government by prescription," and that "there is no other way of obtaining registered title to your property, as the old methods of *Infomracions Posesorias,* etc., were done away with by the Code of Civil Procedure."[202] The regulations that governed obtaining title in this way served to send documents through several offices for final approval and disposition.

The Department of the Interior anticipated that the enormity of the project of correcting imperfect titles and accounting for titles made under Spanish rule would raise the simple question of "Why?" The answer referred back to the relationship between war and archives: "Because all the land records in the Islands, with the exception of three or four provinces, were destroyed and no record exists showing what lands were thus disposed of by the Government."[203] The destruction of records during the wars created the pretext for the implementation of the United States colonial policy of recordkeeping for the disposition of land.

Carabao and "this nefarious organization"

While settling questions of land title in the face of less-than-ideal conditions was sometimes achieved, getting a handle on such recordkeeping did not eliminate other problems appertaining to developing a colonial agricultural economy. The establishment, use, and misuse of a system of registration of brands for cattle, for example, is an example of how social and political conditions in the islands prompted the creation of a system, but how precisely those same conditions enabled negotiation of that system in ways not intended or desired by the colonial administration. That such a well-planned government business of carabao branding was nevertheless open to this exploitation underscores the ingenuity with which people engaged and resisted a system that discounted how the ravages of war made such seemingly simple plans impracticable.

The spread of rinderpest throughout the islands was a persistent problem for people in the Philippines in the first decades of the twentieth century. Just as the colonial administration aggressively sought to survey the arable land in the archipelago and encourage Filipino settlement on tracts previously uninhabited and unfarmed, the islands' carabao—the cattle crucial to agricultural endeavor all over the islands—were dying in droves due to the spreading viral infection. Thus, concurrent with the drive to survey and settle land, the colonial administration prioritized the containment of the disease. The Government Laboratories was established under the purview of the Secretary of the Interior, and the pressure on the government scientists to provide relief was enormous, immediate, and unrelenting.[204]

While the problem of sickness among carabao was well-documented and oft-reported, the problem of carabao theft and the conditions that gave rise to it were less well-known. This difference may be accounted for in the difference in the remaining records on the topics. Whereas the deaths of carabao on such a large scale were significant for the economic development of the islands and therefore reported annually, the problem of carabao theft was, by comparison, quite small.[205] While the government stood to lose money on the spread of rinderpest, those who stood to gain and lose the most from the thefts were not so numerous or powerful to garner much attention. Nevertheless, the emergence of carabao theft came into being as a result of the upheaval of war, military occupation, and the establishment of civil rule, and it provided a glimpse into how archives and recordkeeping could at once enable and document its own undermining.

Philippine Commission Act No. 1147 (May 3, 1904) designated the Bureau of Archives, Patents, Copyrights and Trademarks as the repository of brands for cattle either to be used for work animals or for food, beginning with the 1904-1905 fiscal year. Based on its own records, the bureau estimated 250,000 cattle owners in the islands, in addition to those owned by the colonial government and individuals in areas without municipal governments, namely those territories designated as those of the "non-Christian tribes." The responsibility of registering cattle brands was added to the "unlimited labour, already burdening this office, since the concentration of the notarial protocols and the annexation of the Patents, Copyrights, and Trade-Marks office."[206]

The bureau's work relating to cattle branding had several aspects to it, each presenting particular challenges. The first of these was volume, and another was human error by both applicants and bureau clerks. Hundreds of thousands of brands were to be collected in books made especially for them, which had been distributed to the provincial offices. When these books were filled with brands and reviewed by provincial officers, they would be forwarded to the bureau in Manila for final approval and storage. In principle, such a system would work smoothly even with the large population of cattle owners in the islands, but this turned out not to be the case. Reporting on August 15, 1905, the bureau chief noted that the archives had received brands from 290 municipalities, returned 4,868 for correction, and of those received only 527. In total, the bureau registered

11,236 brands.[207]

Dissatisfaction with the failing system was compounded by the rise in cattle stealing that inadequate documentation, enabled by a loophole in Act No. 1147, made possible. The areas of the Philippines designated as "non-Christian" and the city of Manila were exempted from the requirements of cattle branding, and while the designation of regions in northern Luzon and the southern islands had little effect on cattle stealing, Manila's exemption, its lack of cattle registration laws, and its central location provided means to subvert the bureau's charge of cattle registration.

In the years after the official end of hostilities between United States and Philippine forces, there arose what Executive Secretary A.W. Fergusson termed "this nefarious organization," composed of cattle stealers and cattle owners taking advantage of the disconnect between the records held at the bureau and those of the city of Manila. The scheme went like this: the carabao owner and his accomplice, "the stealer," from province X would agree to allow the "stealer" to take a number of carabao from the owner's property, and register them in Manila under an assumed, agreed-upon name. With these "gilt-edged" papers, the stealer would take the carabao to a neighboring province Y for sale. After some time, the owner of the cattle would go to the neighboring province Y to recover his carabao, identified by his cattle brand registered at the Bureau of Archives, Patents, Copy-rights, and Trademarks under Province X, and upon threat of suing its purchaser for possession of stolen property, would recover his carabao. The owner would have proper claim, because his brand was officially registered with Bureau. The buyer could not know of the scheme, because the papers the stealer presented to him at the time of sale were for a carabao whose brand was officially registered with the city of Manila.[208] This scheme was possible, of course, because the registers of cattle brands in Manila were separate from the registers of provincial cattle brands in the Bureau of Archives, Patents, Copy-rights and Trademarks. If the registers were unified, the carabao would have been discovered as stolen as soon as an attempt was made to register it under an assumed name.

The call for legislation that would bring the registration of cattle in Manila together with registration in the rest of the islands was renewed in the following years. These requests, however, couched in continued accounts of insubordinate provincial offices and the bad press received in the local media, went unheeded until late in 1908. On November 20 of that year, the Municipal Board of the City of Manila passed Ordinance No. 106 to regulate the registration and branding of cattle, thus in part silencing "the clamors of the local press and the complaints of governors of adjoining provinces, which caused so much harm to agriculture in said provinces, as stolen animals were brought to Manila, and due to the defects of procedure in such cases, were easily provided with legal certificates and then shipped to other distant provinces."[209] With the passage of municipal Ordinance No. 106, the circulation of cattle brand registers grew in accordance with the new law. Manila's City Assessor was provided with copies of brands of cattle in the provincial municipalities, townships, and rancherias. And because the ordinance was expected to address the problem of property theft, the Secret Service Department was also furnished with cattle brand registers of the provinces of Bulacan, Cavite, Batangas, Laguna, Tayabas, and Rizal, "in order to enable them to cooperate with the provincial authorities in the arrest of cattle thieves."[210] The systems thought to be perfect for keeping records were thus imperfect, and the streamlining systems ballooned in size. Along these lines, there could flourish a "nefarious organization" designed to steal money from would-be carabao buyers, using precisely the system designed as part of the larger project to get all the elements—land, labor, farm animals—in place for Filipinos' path to prosperity through resettlement and small-scale agriculture.

Conclusion

Still, perhaps the best expression of the United States colonial government's ethos of uniformity was not in the matters of equal population distribution across the islands, the standardized land titles, or cattle-branding, but in the normalizing of geographical names. As would be expected, the creation of a government body to oversee this normalization was concurrent with the beginning years of the Bureau of Lands, the Public Lands Act, and the Land Registration Act. Executive Order 95, signed on November 5, 1903, established a Philippine Committee on Geographical Names. Philippine Commissioner T.H. Pardo de Tavera, Chief of the Bureau of the Bureau of Coast and Geodetic Survey, the Chief of the Bureau of Ethnological Survey, the Chief of Public Lands, the Director of Posts, and Manuel X. Burgos were appointed to the committee, and their duty was to "discharge the same duty in respect to Philippine names as has heretofore been discharged by the Board on Geographical Names appointed by President Harrison in 1890."[211]

The Board on Geographical Names referred to here was a board created by United States President Harrison by Executive Order 27-A, issued September 4, 1890, to decide "cases of disputed nomenclature" in the United States. About fifteen years later, by Executive Order 399 (January 23, 1906), the board's responsibilities were expanded to "include determination, revision, and fixing of geographical names in United States and its insular possessions."[212] Later on that year, the Board on Geographical Names was renamed the United States Geographic Board with the added responsibility of advising the preparation of surveys and maps, and this latter responsibility became that of the Board of Surveys and Maps when it was established in 1919.[213]

In the case of the Philippines, the language of the charge of the Philippine Committee on Geographical Names was, more precisely, to decide "questions of orthography in the spelling of geographic names in the Philippine Archipelago, with a view of securing uniformity of usage throughout the Departments of the Insular Government, and particularly upon maps and charts, issued by its various Bureaus." The uniformity of names was important for the "transaction of public and private business," including the delivery of mail in general and communications with government officials in particular.[214] The committee's decisions were published regularly throughout the beginning years of civil government in the Philippines. The publications included the decided-upon name and spelling of a town, river, mountain, etc., as well as the names and spellings by which it had been known.[215] Determination of uniform geographical names was one element of the colonial state's efforts to standardize its operations. Other efforts included standardizing the way an envelope was addressed, the official channels through which communications should course, the conventional signs for drafting maps, and even what to call, officially, the Philippine Commission in English and in Spanish.[216]

The work of the Philippine Committee on Geographical Names underscores the issues raised by the foregoing discussion of the relationship between the Bureau of Lands and the Bureau of Archives, and of the myriad ways to acquire land under the United States colonial government: the project of documenting the population and the land of the Philippines required careful attention to the details and extent of both. Such simultaneous small- and large-scale thinking and project-planning benefited from, and relied upon, the standardization of single form letters and, subsequently, the near-relentless reproduction and distribution of those letters. What resulted from the mundane and detailed work of the Philippine Committee on Geographical Names and the Bureau of Lands was the core of the colonial archive. The activities resulted in an extensive series of land records, uniform in form and content, thus easily assessed and filed, and documenting a vast expanse of the United States' recently-acquired territory.

Taking all these aspects of the Bureau of Lands together—the cooperation and correspondence with other bureaus, the application processes, and the provisions for legal instruments—the bureau generated an enormous body of records. It was constituted in part by Spanish records and informed by United

States records and served to identify the different parts of the islands. The archives included not only land survey and topographical information, but also came to be filled with announcements from the *Official Gazette* and Spanish and English announcements in the Manila newspapers. This body of records served to identify the many people of the islands, whose names, occupations, addresses, and ancestry were crucial information for the acquisition of land—either by purchase, lease, homestead, or occupation.

Such a mass of records would prove useful when, in 1910 and 1911, the land records of the Philippine Government were required to be brought to the United States by congressional committee charged to investigate the so-called "friar lands controversy." The accused colonial administrators relied on archives sent to Washington, D.C., from Manila to defend themselves. Though a minority of the investigating committee found Worcester, Carpenter, and Forbes at fault, the majority of the investigating committee found them not guilty of wrongdoing. In fact, the committee's reading of the archives showed them to be patriotic in the execution of their duty, of trying to sell large tracts of lands in the Philippines to reduce the colonial government's indebtedness to, of all things, the United States government. Thus the records that the Bureau of Land had generated in its first decade to document its activities also elucidated the meaning and limits of the Land Registration Laws, and eventually helped to exonerate the colonial administration of the charge that it violated the United States policy of "Benevolent Assimilation."

The difference between the military and civil government in the Philippines was defined by a difference of political opinion between United States military forces and Governor-General Taft. The necessity of resolving this, and more to the point, pacifying the revolution in the Philippines had consequences for public land laws of the Philippines. The major point of disagreement about land legislation, which made it so contentious in both the Philippines and the United States, was the question of whether the rapid influx of foreign capital to the islands would be good or bad for the Filipinos. Throughout the American colonial period in the Philippines, the rules and regulations for land ownership continued to be the topic of discussion. This was especially true as the colonial government struggled to attain some measure of prosperity, or at least the conditions for prosperity. Though there was ongoing disagreement about the utility of its restrictions, the land registration law was ultimately successful in at least one important, insidious, and enduring aspect. It was cause for the consultation, assessment and ultimate displacement of the Spanish system of land recordkeeping, part of the general project of American occupation of the Philippines. It precipitated the establishment of an American system of recordkeeping, the creation of a new archive of land records.

The creation of uniform, far-reaching, centralized recordkeeping and archival retrieval systems were central to the effort to develop the islands' colonial economy. It was also central to an economy of effort insofar as the work of the bureaucrats at the Bureau of Lands and Bureau of Archives was concerned. Throughout the first two decades of United States' colonial rule of the Philippines, despite carefully-crafted legislation and the development of forms and procedure, the ideal of settling islanders on theretofore uncultivated, arable land was not realized. Indeed, even as the Philippine Committee on Geographical Names labored to make the names of towns, rivers and mountains uniform, the people living there remained unruly.

CHAPTER 5
CONCLUSION

> One fact must be conceded in studying the Philippine question: The Filipinos are *a people*, like the Cubans or the Irish or the French—a distinct political entity, with a consciousness of kind and with national feelings and aspirations, no matter how poorly developed they may be in some directions. Once this fact is conceded, the real issue to be dealt with then becomes not the success or failure of American experiments in the Islands or the fitness of the Filipinos to establish American institutions, but the relations that should exist between the American people and the Filipino people.
>
> --Maximo Kalaw, 1916[217]

By 1913, the so-called "Taft Era" was over, Governor Woodrow Wilson had captured the United States Presidency, and U.S. Congressman Francis Burton Harrison (D-NY) was appointed to the office of the Governor-General of the Philippine Islands. Given these new developments in the United States, every action of the Philippine colonial administration—for better or worse—was understood in light of Harrison's early opposition in Congress to the United States' imperialist policies toward the Philippines. The most important of the changes in U.S.-Philippine relations at the time was the passage of the Philippine Autonomy Act on August 29, 1916.

Also known as the Jones Act, this law led to the establishment of the Philippine Senate as the upper house of the colonial legislature, ushering in a new era of Philippine governance. Until that point, most political power was concentrated in the Philippine Commission, membership of which was constituted by appointment—initially by the President of the United States and later by the Governor-General of the Philippines. From the establishment of civil government until 1907, the Philippine Commission had served as the entirety of both the executive and legislative branches of the Philippine government, with members serving as both lawmakers and cabinet members. In 1907, this monopoly was somewhat broken by the establishment of the Philippine Assembly. It marked the beginning of a bicameral legislative branch in the islands, with Filipinos serving in the newly-established elected lower house and the Philippine Commission continuing to serve as the upper house. With the passage of the Jones Act and the establishment of the Philippine Senate as the upper house in 1916, the Philippine Commission served only as part of the executive branch and the legislative function of colonial government was made bicameral and the responsibility of Filipinos. This was the centerpiece of the general policy of Filipinization and a nod to Filipinos' capacity to self-govern.[218]

Thus the publication of Maximo Kalaw's *The Case for the Filipinos* in 1916 was well-timed. He began by dismissing the two questions that dominated United State-Philippine relations: whether people of the Philippines wanted independence, and whether they could handle it. Paradoxically, to Kalaw, it was these questions that circumscribed the possibility of seriously discussing the "relations that should exist between the American people and the Filipino people." Kalaw's analysis of the discourse on United States colonialism between 1898 to 1916 was remarkable because it was an astute reading of the present and recent past through which he was living. It was also noteworthy because it ran counter to an enormous body of work—generated by the colonial government, its unofficial organs, and even its opponents—that fixated on the question of Filipino aspirations and capacity.

Secretary of the Interior Dean Worcester's public lectures so consistently addressed purported Filipino incapacity and American ingenuity that Kalaw could very well have cited any number of Worcester's works. For the purpose of appreciating the role that colonial government archives played in facilitating Worcester's arguments, it is helpful to suppose that Kalaw could very well have been thinking of "Conditions in the Philippines," a speech delivered by Worcester at a banquet in his honor at the Manila Hotel in 1913 before the publication of his *The Philippines Past and Present*. In a typical moment of unchecked self-promotion, Worcester noted that his analysis was based on six months of "a careful reading of the records of the Insurgent Government" that allowed him to authoritatively report, "in no uncertain terms," on the government, "basing [his] conclusions on evidence which cannot be controverted, to-wit, its official records."[219] Kalaw's summary analysis of colonialist discourse was, without naming names, a critique of Worcester's uncritical use of "evidence"—seized, translated, and arranged by the United States military during his tenure in the Philippines—to make his point about Filipino incapacity, based on records complementary to his own.[220]

Though Dean Worcester could be relied upon to reproduce—with zeal and consistency—the arguments of which Kalaw was critical, Worcester was not the only colonial administrator who used his special access to government records to write enduring, laudatory historical accounts of the United States' rule in the islands. Immediately after having served on the Philippine Commission and returned to the United States, for example, Bernard Moses made contact with his former employer to request copies of the commission's minutes, so that he could write "an account of the establishment of civil government in the Philippines" that provided an alternative viewpoint from that offered by the commercial press.[221] Another former Philippine Commissioner, David Barrows, published his first account of United States rule in the Philippines, *A History of the Philippines*, in 1905 for use in Philippine schools, and a second edition of the textbook was published in 1914. In both cases, Barrows described his sources and how he was able to find them—namely, thanks to the courtesy of Philippine Commissioner Pardo de Tavera who allowed Barrows to use his private library and Bureau of Archives Chief Manuel Yriarte who granted him access to public documents.[222] These connections appear to have continued to serve Barrows well, as his description of sources consulted in the writing of *A Decade of American Government in the Philippines, 1903-1913* specifies his use of government documents in the colony (Philippine Commission reports, bureau reports, reports of secretaries of executive departments, reports of the Military Governors, laws passed by the Philippine Commission) as well as some from the United States (testimony before the U.S. Senate in 1902).[223] Whether it was bombastic Worcester on the lecture circuit with his infamous lantern slides, faltering Bernard Moses with his would-be answer to the commercial press in Manila, or prolific David Barrows with a readership of Filipino schoolchildren and curious Americans—all were former colonial officials whose access to records of the colonial government facilitated the arguments that Kalaw sought to defuse.

Indeed, by the time of *The Case for the Filipino*'s publication, Kalaw had at his disposal hundreds of articles, essays, and monographs on the United States' occupation of the Philippines. Those that supported the United States' colonial occupation—such as works by Worcester, Moses, and Barrows—followed a pattern of argumentation so consistently that Kalaw could parse the works composed over the course of two decades in a few sentences:

> The ordinary course taken in the discussion of the Philippine problem is this: If the writer be an advocate of Philippine retention, after hastily disposing, in his first few pages, of Philippine acquisition as an inevitable God-sent incident of the Spanish-American War, he usually devotes the rest of his work to an exhaustive discussion of American achievements in the Islands, the improvements in education, roads, and public buildings, the extension of sanitary measures, and the fostering of commerce and industry; belittling, ignoring, or denying the cooperation given by the Filipinos in accomplishing these results; often depicting them in the darkest colors, if not, indeed, flagrantly misrepresenting them, ridiculing their characteristics, exploiting their supposed ignorance, and exaggerating, if not entirely creating anew, native vices and shortcomings. He, too, often, takes the greatest pains to expose the mistakes of some locality or the crimes of some individual, and, by adroit innuendoes, indicates them as the prevailing tendencies of the Filipinos. Nothing in such volumes is spared to prejudice the American people against the Filipinos, so that he may close

the volume with the conclusion that American domination must continue indefinitely and that Philippine independence, if any such thing ever be possible, is yet a long way off.[224]

Kalaw's pithy observation that the United States' acquisition of the Philippines was immediately and hastily explained "as an inevitable God-sent incident of the Spanish-American War" is also wry. He underscored that for proponents of United States retention of the islands, the crux of the matter was already, satisfactorily sorted out. How should the peoples of the United States and the Philippines relate? The Philippines should remain a dependency of the United States, they concluded. Discussions of whether certain colonial projects took hold and whether other colonial experiments were successful, to Kalaw's mind, equivocated. They took for granted the condition of colonial occupation that enabled the United States' sundry projects and experiments.

With regard to works by proponents of Philippine independence, Kalaw noted that they tended to make "a much more appreciative study of the Philippine Government, established at Malolos," before detailing all the many ways Filipinos were prepared for immediate independence. By categorizing the writings on the Philippines under United States rule in one of two ways before proceeding with his case for Philippine independence, Kalaw at once read along and against the grain, acknowledging the dominant discourse before turning to propose an alternative model. In so doing, while the prize may seem to have been immediate independence, this was not the only measure of achievement. At stake, too, was the disavowal of the colonial project's value—a shift away from discussions centered on the success and failure of American experiments in the Islands.

The archives and archives-in-the-making of the colonial state were integral to the United States' military operations in the Philippines, as well as to its later civil projects. The work of American personnel to survey Spanish archives during the Philippine-American War assisted in the determination of the United States as the sovereign of the Philippines. The work to create an anti-imperialist alternative to the government's documentation of the war illustrated both the battle of public opinion and attention to posterity, while the work to assess and record the extent and conditions of land was integral to remaking the archipelago's economy and entrenching the colonial state. Whether assisting the United States' interest in regard to war, public opinion, commerce, or governance, the Bureau of Archives and its later iterations were centrally situated in the colonial government, an important administrative functionary in the United States' rule in the islands. Thus, Kalaw's analysis of how retentionists dwelled on colonialism's "achievements" mark an important shift in the use of the colonial government's records.

In other words, the end of the so-called Taft Era and the end of the tenure of the first cohort of American colonial administrators marked a beginning. Relieved administrators reflected on and wrote accounts of the United States' first fifteen years of Philippine occupation. These accounts made use of the inactive records housed in the Bureau of Archives and active records made available to them by former colleagues. Though the number of researchers provided with access to the records was limited, as was perhaps the extent of records made available to them, it allowed for the continued production of writing on the Philippines after the initial excitement of annexation had waned, novel insofar as it was authored by former colonial officials who demanded a kind of authority on account of their involvement in the establishment of the colonial government.

To put it another way, once the civil government was securely in place and its records became the source material that further secured colonialist arguments for the continued occupation of the islands, the archives became a more explicitly public and legitimating entity than it had been previously. With the islands' first Reorganization Act, (Act No. 1407, October 26, 1905), the Bureau of Archives helped establish the civil governance of the islands, when archives was merged with the Bureau of Patents, Copyrights, and Trademarks to become the Division of Archives, Patents, Copyrights and Trademarks. Also, the entire unit was moved from the Department of Public Instruction to the Executive Bureau. These changes highlighted the archive's increasingly important role in the economic development of the islands, as the archives expanded its utility by becoming the repository for legal instruments relating to the development of that land.

A decade after the first Reorganization Act, the Philippine Assembly passed another Reorganization Act, Act No. 2572 (February 4, 1916).[225] Theretofore certainly the most wide-reaching legislation in terms of the government's archives, this law considerably changed the scope and structure of the Division of Archives, Patents, Copyrights, and Trade-Marks. The division was transferred to the Department of Public Instruction from the Executive Bureau, and it was consolidated with the Philippine Library and the Law and Library Division of the Philippine Assembly. This consolidation resulted in the creation of the Philippine Library and Museum. The Department of Public Instruction's administration of the Philippine Library and Museum was short-lived. Shortly after the passage of the Jones Act, the Philippine Library and Museum was transferred to the Department of Justice on December 18, 1916.[226] Whether within the Department of Public Instruction or the Department of Justice, the archives were no longer grouped with the records that supported economic activity. Rather than being assembled with patents, copyrights, and trademarks, the archives were part of a unit comprised of libraries and a museum. The changes affected by the re-organization were the recasting of the organization and open access to records documenting the past.

For those opposed to the United States' presence in the Philippines, one additional benefit of this access to the archives is evidenced by Kalaw's analysis of unapologetically, irrepressibly laudatory depictions of the United States achievements in the Philippines. Accounts of American benevolence were no longer only originating from colonial administrations' partisan supporters, but from the colonial administration's own alumni. This being the case, the connection between praise and indefinite retention was easy to draw and—as Kalaw did—critique.

Thus, the archives not only continued to serve an administrative function but also became a resource for researchers, marking a shift in purpose and audience. Whereas it had served a primarily economic service from its establishment, after the 1916 creation of the Philippine Library and Museum, its primary role was to provide a cultural service. Indeed, the establishment of the Philippine Library and Museum in 1916, per Act No. 2572, was the result of the merger of three organizations. Two of the three organizations (the Law and Library Division was the exception) were themselves the result of previous mergers. The Museum of Ethnology, Natural History and Commerce had within it two sizable departments, the Museum of Ethnology and the Commercial Museum, and the Philippine Library had been formed in 1910 with the consolidation of several government libraries. Thus, the creation of the Philippine Library and Museum was the capstone consolidation for these many predecessor organizations.[227]

This change in purpose was especially clear after 1918, when the responsibilities appertaining to patents, copyrights, and trademarks were transferred to the new commerce department. Also, the shift to a broader audience was coupled with the fact that the archives' administrators reported to new leadership. From the end of the Spanish period and well into the United States period in the Philippines, the archives had been under the administration of Spaniard Manuel Yriarte—whether the archives was a division or a bureau, whether in the Executive Bureau or the Department of Education. Still, even with all of these changes, throughout the first two decades of United States rule of the Philippines, Yriarte reported to an American administrator. After the 1916 creation of the Philippine Library and Museum, not only was the Bureau of Archives obliged to orient itself outwards; its leadership was obliged to report to a Filipino for the first time ever. Indeed, if the structural change to the archive altered its primary audience, the individual change in leadership altered the situation as well, in the post-Jones Act Philippines.

CONCLUSION

***

"I feel it is just a monument to wasted endeavor."
--Syrena McKee, on the Philippine Library and Museum, 1919[228]

The archives' shift in audience, purpose, and leadership may initially seem to be a minor matter, but to accept it as such would be to continue the elision of the archives' significant role in the economic development of the islands. Syrena McKee's dismissal of the Philippine Library and Museum, shared privately with former director of the Philippine Library James Robertson in 1919, illustrates another way that the work of the archives in colonial rule could be obscured: it was a failed institution, no longer dynamic and unworthy of further investment or attention. She described the staffing changes with a touch of either wistfulness or bitterness, noting that one American colleague was leaving the Philippines because she was "at the end of her tether," another was "obliged" to leave, and a third would be gone very shortly. She recounted these departures and also noted that a newspaper account of the history of the library did not include any mention of American librarians, namely Robertson, herself, and Emma Osterman Elmer.[229]

Syrena McKee had been on staff at the Philippine Library, under James Robertson's direction. In 1916, with the creation of the Philippine Library and Museum and the appointment of Teodoro Kalaw (brother of Maximo Kalaw) as director, Robertson elected to leave his position. In the years following Robertson's departure, McKee sent periodical letters to Robertson, describing the political situation in the library that resulted with the change in leadership and discussed issues of appointments and staffing.[230] Writing about the Philippine Library and Museum in 1919, however, McKee did not equivocate. She noted simply that she felt the place to be "just a monument to wasted endeavor." To her mind, the decline of the organization in the three years since the passage of the Jones Act was unmistakable and precipitous.

In the context of the Philippines after the inauguration of Governor-General Francis Burton Harrison in 1913, McKee's bitter assessment may not seem remarkable. Harrison was a well-known opponent of the United States' policy in the Philippines and, therefore, was praised and welcomed by some Americans and Filipinos alike. According to Maximo Kalaw, Resident Commissioner Manuel Quezon considered his work to secure Harrison's appointment "his greatest personal triumph in America."[231] Reflecting on his general support of the Harrison administration and its policy of Filipinization, colonial administrator Walter William Marquardt simply observed that, "It seems to me that there are a number of Americans whose services can as well be dispensed with, and that there are a number of Filipinos who should be promoted to higher positions."[232] Major-General J.F. Bell reported that he had "not talked with anyone who, having come in personal contact with the Governor-General, was not favorably impressed by him. He is universally considered a most kind, considerate, courteous, able and conservative man."[233]

Even those Americans averse to recognizing Filipino capacity whatsoever had to acknowledge the change. Writing to George Harvey after Woodrow Wilson's successful campaign for the United States presidency, Harry Bandholtz ruefully observed that "The possible passage of the Jones Bill at the next or some early session of Congress [...] has wrought our little protégés here into a considerable frenzy."[234] In the spring of 1914, a dispute about the dismissal of American employees in the colonial government found voice in the *New York Times*. When Worcester weighed in on the debate, he argued that Harrison had inaugurated "a policy under which experienced and competent Americans in very large numbers have been forced out of the service or have left it in disgust, and their places have been filled with Filipinos, some of whom are well known to be incompetent, while others are as yet untried"; Worcester concluded that "Disaster will inevitably follow the continuance of such a policy, and already begins to loom ominously."[235]

For his part, William Howard Taft attributed the islands' financial troubles, especially as they related to the friar lands, to the replacement of Charles Sleeper with Manuel Tinio as Director of the Bureau of Lands, a change presumed to be made per the policy of Filipinization. Other officials, including James Alexander Robertson before he left the service, shared their criticisms of Harrison with Worcester, who offered a most sympathetic ear.[236] Privately, in a letter to Secretary of War Garrison, the outgoing Governor-General W. Cameron Forbes predicted that Quezon himself would turn against Harrison. He wrote

> There could not be anything more dangerous to the peace and welfare of the Islands than to have Quezon think he can run the Governor-General and make and unmake him. Thus, if the experience of the past goes for anything, he will very shortly undertake to dictate who shall be appointed, then turn against Governor Harrison as he has against me.[237]

Forbes seems to have relished the controversy he stirred on the eve of his departure.[238] The predictable complaints drew on the well-rehearsed low estimations of Filipino capacity. Opponents of Philippine independence simply read doom in aggressive Filipinization.

CONCLUSION

Thus what makes McKee's evaluation of the Philippine Library and Museum worth considering further is the fact that it should also be understood in the general context of this hostility to Filipinization, as well the specific context of the change in the purpose and audience of the colonial state's archives. McKee's letters focus on the functions and staff with which Robertson would have been familiar, as well as the intrigue surrounding Kalaw's appointment. Though McKee's sense of the situation cannot be necessarily accepted as the prevailing view about the administration of the Philippine Library and Museum or of the archives, it does suggest misgivings about the role Filipinos began to take in the major cultural organization of the Philippine government.

In view of this, McKee's feeling that the institution was a "monument to wasted endeavor" is not as simple as it first seems and indeed addresses the ways the institution figured into the political context of the islands. To accept United States colonial rule on its own purported terms was to accept the notion that Filipinos were under American tutelage and had the capacity to learn to govern themselves to some degree. With the transition in organization and leadership to the divisions within the Philippine Library and Museum, an assessment of successful tutelage might have read, "monument to worthwhile endeavor." As it was, however, McKee held the administration of the Philippine Library and Museum in low esteem and viewed its poor management to be the unfortunate conclusion to the Americans' hard work. In short, she suggested that they had tried to teach the Filipinos lessons but had failed.

Another way to read McKee's assessment is to understand her to mean that any institution transferred out of American administrators' purview signaled a waste of effort, because the "endeavor" was not instruction of Filipinos but indefinite retention of the Philippines. This would indicate adherence to a strain of thinking that rejected Filipinos' capacity to govern themselves. Thus, the Philippine Library and Museum would not be a monument to either wasted or worthwhile endeavor—never a monument, it would be an institution continuously in the making. In this light, they had tried to keep the Philippines but had failed.

Either way of understanding "a monument to wasted endeavor" suggests dissatisfaction with the changes to the library and archives. The Philippine Library and Museum was not immune to the questions of Filipino capacity, implicit in McKee's letter to Robertson and explicit in Kalaw's *Case for the Filipinos*. Indeed, such questions obscured the question that Kalaw identified as most pressing, namely the question of relations between the United States and the Philippines.

At the same time, the question of Filipino capacity highlighted tension between American and Filipino workers, and such tension further obscured the role of the archives, as it became just another site where Filipino capacity was tested. Thus, the questions of Filipino capacity obscured the purpose that the archive had served in the first two decades of American rule, as if the expansion of the bureaus expressly designated for economic expansion was not enough to obscure.

***

> "The public records now in the Philippines will have a special interest to this country [...]."
>
> Librarian of Congress Herbert Putnam, 1903[239]

At the end of the nineteenth century, the archives of the Philippines did indeed "have a special interest" to the United States. With the acquisition of the Philippines, the archives were necessary for learning the most basic information about the islands and their people, and they were certainly needed for assessing the threat of the revolutionary government, the extent and condition of the annexed lands, and the people who might be convinced to work on them. In the first two decades of United States colonial rule of the Philippines, the archives were flexible in serving these purposes. Also throughout this period, several factors worked to obscure the work of the archives.

The first factor was limited access to records, most broadly defined. Indeed, limited access to records characterizes every example offered in this study. During the Philippine-American War, the United States military sought to capture any documents of the new Philippine Republic, and the Anti-Imperialist League was eager for greater access to United States government documents and busy creating their own. With the worst of the hostilities over, the Philippine Commission established the Bureau of Archives within four months of civil government having been established, in an effort to track down and centralize the records of the ousted Spanish regime. Alongside the records of the new regime, these documents became of keen interest to American historians whose use of the records was restricted. The challenges to the resettlement of Filipinos onto uncultivated land were numerous and complex, and among them were the matters of determining the extent of land and reaching people who might make a formal application. Whether it was failed attempts of organizations to access other organizations' restricted records or stilted efforts of individuals to access records that were new and foreign, getting at the documentation and making sense of it was easier said than done. Only some people could see and use the archives.

Second and paradoxically, the overwhelming volume of records that were in the care of the Bureau of Archives (and the Bureau of Insular Affairs) had the same consequences as did limited access to records. The enormous volume of records complicated the work that the archives was designed to do and obscured the work that it did do. The early reports of the Bureau of Archives reliably rehearse the unit's woes of limited storage space, less than ideal physical conditions, and records in disarray. With the bureau's expansion to include patents, copyrights, and trademarks, the volume of records—including those many forms completed erroneously—increased considerably, as did work associated with their care. One measure of the burden on the archives was the increase in requests for copies of the material. According to annual reports from the bureau, the numbers increased every year (336 copies in 1903, 580 in 1904, and 623 in 1905). In 1905, that many copies translated into 894,694 words. By 1907, 1,497 copies were made totaling 1,248, 802. Executive Secretary A.W. Fergusson opened his 1907 report on the archives, understating that

> The great amount of work involved in the licensing of foreign corporations and in the issuance of certificates of incorporation, added to the duties heretofore performed by this division, viz., furnishing certified copies of notarial documents in the former archives of the Spanish Government, the registration of patents, copyrights, and trademarks, and of cattle brands for all large cattle throughout the islands, has made this division a very busy one throughout the fiscal year just ended.[240]

The surveys and other records of the Bureau of Lands over-corrected for its initial lack of records with its aggressive creation of replacements for missing Spanish records and revisions of Spanish records found wanting. The purpose of gathering so much information, of course, was to facilitate the growth and operation of the new government, but in regard to the work of the archive, the volumes of material resulting from such aggressive efforts made it difficult to see. Once able to gain access to the records, their physical extent, sometimes coupled with inconsistency and disarray, made it difficult to observe their larger function for the United States' imperial ambitions and, indeed, even for the everyday business of the colonial government in the Philippines.

Within that government, of course, the Bureau of Archives was not the only unit working diligently. All of the other units had specific charges in service of colonial governance, and while the periodic reorganization of these units throughout the first twenty years of colonial rule does not make a chronicle of the archives impossible, neither does the archive's re-assignment within different bureaus and divisions of the Philippine government make the chronicle simple. Moreover, because in 1916, the Bureau of Archives ended up in the Philippine Library and

Museum, the most expected of places, it would be easy and not unreasonable to suppose that it had a relatively direct route from its founding to the library and museum. Thus, a third factor obscuring the work of the Bureau of Archives in the United States colonial project was the common sense of its placement within the colonial government after the 1916 reorganization, and the challenges of piecing together an institutional history to know otherwise.

Finally, the role of the archives in the early years of the United States occupation was later obscured by the growth of the bureaus it had initially supported. The Civil Service Board, Bureau of Labor, Bureau of Public Lands, and Bureau of Archives were all organized at around the same time, and their successful operation depended upon regular and active collaboration. As hostilities between United States and Philippine forces subsided, the institutions of the new colonial government had room to thrive. Soon, the Bureau of Archives was less needed to provide support to the other bureaus of the colonial government. For the most part, its job was done.

***

> The archivist thus may be regarded as a hewer of wood and a drawer of water for the scholars. [...] The archivist's job at all times is to preserve the evidence, impartially, without taint of political or ideological bias, so that on the basis of this evidence those judgments may be pronounced upon men and events by prosperity which historians through human failings are momentarily incapable of pronouncing. Archivists are thus the guardians of the truth, or, at least, of the evidence on the basis of which truth can be established.
>
> --Theodore Roosevelt Schellenberg, *Modern Archives: Principles and Techniques*, 1956 [241]

The primary goal of this work has been to demonstrate the important political role that the colonial state's archive played in the United States' rule of the Philippines between 1898 and 1916. In examining the relationship between the archive and specific facets of the United States' policy of "Benevolent Assimilation," I have suggested several of the forces that drove and shaped the growth of the Bureau of Archives and its later iterations. It has taken another perspective on the truism that government documents alone ought not to be taken at face value and ought not to be presumed to present a full, complex picture of any situation, by showing that critique of the available sources is as old as the formal relationship between the United States and the Philippines. In short, this book primarily makes a particular historical argument: in the context of the United States' rule of the Philippines, if roads were supposed to bring economic development, schools were supposed to mold model citizens; civil service regulations were supposed to yield skilled laborers, and a bicameral legislature was supposed to transform natives into self-governable subjects, the initial and primary purpose of the colonial state's archive was to facilitate those projects not only through documentation but also with other administrative support.

A related, secondary goal of this work has been to contribute to a rather muted conversation within today's archival studies scholarship. Without a doubt, practicing archivists and scholars in archival studies are well aware of, and quite attentive to, the ways in which an organization's internal culture and external political conditions can affect the establishment, maintenance, and development of an archival institution because these issues shape present-day best practice. Likewise, practicing archivists and scholars in archival studies are mindful of the way that past political conditions can affect their collections. Considering all of these works together—those that take seriously the impact of the present and past political context on best practice—there appears to emerge a gap that this book attempts to highlight and to begin to fill.

In other words, this work's specific, historical argument raises questions for archival training and practice today. To be more precise, in the United States, archivists understand that the government archive in a democracy ideally provides accountability and transparency to the people it serves. Such thinking is fundamentally changed, however, when the United States' government archive is in fact a colonial government archive. In the context of the Philippines between 1898 and 1916, the archive's administrators were not documenting a government accountable to Filipinos who had voted all of the islands' leaders into power. Rather they were documenting a government accountable to the leaders in the United States who had appointed officials to impose a colonial state. This circumstance begs the question: what does it mean to be a good archivist and gather, arrange, and describe—that is, to follow the seemingly endless directives of the colonial administration?

When framed in this way, the answer must be, as it was in the Philippines: to be a good archivist insofar as dutifully observing the colonial administration's directives is to actively entrench and maintain that colonial administration. To be a good archivist is to do the everyday, humdrum work of keeping up a government that was not "benevolent." As with all historical arguments, from the perspective of the present-day, any judgment of these past practices may be charged of presentism, of assessing an historical situation by today's standards or value. The point of this study, however, is to put the institution in historical context, and it has found that the activities of the colonial government archive were indeed subject to critique, sometimes scathing even then.

Even if such an allegation of presentism is conceded, and this work accepts that critique of past acts is "unfair," the question of present day practice is nevertheless raised. That is, even if it is conceded that archivists in the United States' government archive in the Philippines were acting in accordance with their own senses of professional and ethical duty (as neither was yet outlined for the then only-emerging science) at the same time that it is accepted that the United States' policy of "Benevolent Assimilation" was a centerpiece in the history of American exceptionalism—critiqued by some Americans at the beginning of the twentieth century and more readily critiqued now at the beginning of the twenty-first century—archivists must at least consider how present practice helps to maintain whatever "invisible," unquestioned, or readily-accepted order. While such a question may never make it into a profession-wide discussion of professional ethics, it undoubtedly returns archivists to the claim that the work of archives can never be conducted outside of ideology.

Finally, and most importantly, this book suggests that these two arguments—one historical, another applied—are in fact, two parts of a single argument about the relationship between scholarship and practice. An historical account of the creation of an archive serves as a reminder to historians and archivists of the times when they were not so removed from one another, but in fact, worked collaboratively to create institutions and bodies of scholarship for the United States, then an emergent world power. Certainly, this reminder is not made to valorize those efforts. Rather, it is made to note that archives came from somewhere. They were made in specific historical contexts, under particular political pressures, with concrete material consequences. They are not unchanging, immovable. Quite to the contrary, they are made and remade, as needed, contentiously, again and again.

ENDNOTES

1. Turner, Frederick Jackson. *The Frontier in American History.* New York: Holt, Rinehart, and Winston, [1893] 1965.

2. William McKinley to the Secretary of War, Dec. 21, 1898, "Message from the President of the United States," 56th Cong., 1st Sess., 1899-1900, S. Doc. 208, 82-83.

3. Teodoro A. Agoncillo, *History of the Filipino People* (Quezon City: Garotech Publishing, 1990), 190; Renato Constantino, *The Philippines: A Past Revisited* (Quezon City: Tala Publishing Services, 1975), 199.

4. David J. Silbey, *A War of Frontier and Empire: The Philippine-American War, 1899-1902* (New York: Hill and Wang, 2006), 165.

5. Stephen Kinzer, *Overthrow: America's Century of Regime Change from Hawaii to Iraq* (New York: Times Books, 2006), 53.

6. Paul Kramer, "The Water Cure," *New Yorker* (February 25, 2008).

7. For analysis of depictions of Filipinos in the United States media, see: Servando D. Halili, Jr., *Iconography of the New Empire: Race and Gender Images and the American Colonization of the Philippines* (Quezon City: University of the Philippines Press, 2006). For analysis of how United States soldiers saw Filipinos, see: Russell Roth, *Muddy Glory: America's 'Indian Wars' in the Philippines, 1899-1935* (West Hanover, MA: The Christopher Publishing House, 1981); and "Stuart Creighton Miller, "The American Soldier and the Conquest of the Philippines" in *Reappraising an Empire: New Perspectives on Philippine-American History* (Cambridge: Harvard University Press, 1984), 13-34.

8. On the challenges to "uplift," see: Matthew Frye Jacobson, *Barbarian Virtues: The United States Encounters Foreign Peoples at Home and Abroad, 1876-1917* (New York: Hill and Wang, 2000), 226; on the mutually constituting racial identities, see: Paul Kramer, *The Blood of Government: Race, Empire, the United States and the Philippines* (Chapel Hill: University of North Carolina Press), 89-90.

9. Reynaldo Ileto, *Knowing America's Colony: A Hundred Years from the Philippine War* (Honolulu: University of Hawai'i Center for Philippines Studies, 1999), 22.

10. Ibid, 30.

11. Warwick Anderson, *Colonial Pathologies: American Tropical Medicine, Race, and Hygiene in the Philippines* (Durham: Duke University Press, 2006), 71. See also: Reynaldo

Ileto, "Cholera and the origins of the American sanitary order in the Philippines" in *Imperial Medicine and Indigenous Societies* (New York: Manchester University Press, 1988), 125-148 and Rodney Sullivan, "Cholera and colonialism in the Philippines, 1899-1903" in *Disease, Medicine, and Empire* (New York: Routledge, 1988), 284-300.

12. Vicente Rafael, *White Love and Other Events in Filipino History* (Durham: Duke University Press, 2000), 28.

13. Ibid, 32. Benito M. Vergara, Jr. writes of the 1903 Census that, "The controlled movement of educated Filipino bodies across the landscape, while shepherded by American officials, would have been important to the rigorous deployment and display of power within the colonial context." Benito M. Vergara, Jr., *Displaying Filipinos: Photography and Colonialism in Early 20th Century Philippines* (Quezon City: University of the Philippines Press, 1995), 47.

14. Ruby Paredes, ed., *Philippine Colonial Democracy* (New Haven, CT: Yale University Southeast Asia Studies, 1988), 1. She suggests that if the Philippines had been a settlement colony, rather than a conquest colony, the possibility of colonial democracy may have been realized (2).

15. Nicholas Thomas, *Colonialism's Culture: Anthropology, Travel, and Government* (Princeton, NJ: Princeton University Press, 1994).

16. Michael Adas, "Improving on the Civilizing Mission? Assumptions of United States Exceptionalism in the Colonization of the Philippines" in Eds. Lloyd C. Gardner and Marilyn B. Young, *The New American Empire: A 21st Century Teach-In on U.S. Foreign Policy* (New York: The New Press, 2005), 162.

17. Romeo V. Cruz, *America's Colonial Desk in the Philippines, 1898-1934* (Quezon City: University of the Philippines Press, 1974), 19.

18. Warwick Anderson, "Where Every Prospect Pleases and Only Man Is Vile: Laboratory Medicine as Colonial Discourse," *Critical Inquiry* 18 (Spring 1992): 506-529; Patricio N. Abinales, "Progressive-Machine Conflict in Early-Twentieth-Century U.S. Politics and Colonial State Building in the Philippines," in Eds. Julian Go and Anne L. Foster, *The American Colonial State in the Philippines: Global Perspectives* (Manila: Anvil, 2005), 148-181.

19. Glenn Anthony May, *Social Engineering in the Philippines: The Aims, Execution, and Impact of American Colonial Policy, 1900-1913* (Westport, CT: Greenwood Press, 1980), xvii.

20. Ibid, 183. The second essay of this exam will discuss the work of May and his critics more fully, with special attention to Reynaldo Ileto's "History and Criticism: The Invention of Heroes" in *Filipinos and their Revolution: Event, Discourse, and Historiography* (Quezon City: Ateneo de Manila University Press, 1998),203-37.

21. Norman G. Owen, "Introduction: Philippine Society and American Colonialism" in *Compadre Colonialism: Philippine-American Relations: 1898-1946* (Manila: Solidaridad, [1971?]), 3.

22. Michael Cullinane, "Implementing the "New Order": The Structure and Supervision of Local Government During the Taft Era" in *Compadre Colonialism: Philippine-American Relations: 1898-1946* (Manila: Solidaridad, [1971?]), 27. See also: Fr. Rolando S. Delagoza, *History of the Philippine Civil Service* (Manila: Rex Printing Company, 1991), 28-29.

23. Stoler, Ann Laura. *Along the Archival Grain: Epistemic Anxieties and Colonial Common Sense.* Princeton, NJ: Princeton University Press, 2010.

24. Watterson's observations continued: "It is not only the great newspapers and the news-gathering associations that are to be considered. These sent experienced correspondents and observers capable of describing and understanding great events, but there was also a real "army" of correspondents of the "home papers." Every regiment and company had its enlisted reporter or correspondent, whose letters to the town or village paper will lend a new interest to the history of war. And all these reported the opinion of the general movement or the great events. Then, all the newspapers were deluged with private letters from soldiers to their families at home. The intelligence of the United States was writing the history of the war it was prosecuting. Only the archives of the Navy, War, and State Departments are to be opened to complete the material." Henry Watterson, *History of the Spanish-American War* (New York: The Werner Company, 1898), 587-88.

25. Treaty of Paris, U.S.-Spain, Dec. 10, 1898, http://avalon.law.yale.edu/19th_century/sp1898.asp.

26. Report of the Bureau of Archives, Philippine Commission Report (1901), RG 350, NACP.

27. Ibid.

28. Exhibit AA: Spanish Records in the Provinces was appended to the Report of the Chief of the Bureau of 10n 1904 and 190101, RG 350, NACP. Archives, a part of the Philippine Commission Report, 1901, RG 350, NACP.

29. Ibid. For reports of District Commanders, see box 1, Records of the United States Army Overseas Operations and Commands, 1898-1942, RG 395, NAB. Some, but

doubtfully all, of the reports of District Commanders are held at the National Archives and Records Administration in Washington, D.C. They, like the archives reported on therein, are time-worn, bug-eaten, or otherwise physically compromised.

30. Robertson to Executive Secretary, Nov. 12, 1912, file 702, RG 350, NACP.

31. Report of the Bureau of Archives, Philippine Commission Report (1901), RG 350, NACP.

32. Ibid.

33. Ford would later enjoy a long career at the Massachusetts Historical Society. Louis Leonard Tucker, *Worthington Chauncey Ford: Scholar and Adventurer* (Boston: Northeastern University Press, 2001).

34. A. Curtis Wilgus, "The Life of James Alexander Robertson" in *Hispanic American Essays: A Memorial to James Alexander Robertson,* ed. A. Curtis Wilgus (Chapel Hill: The University of North Carolina Press, 1942), 3-9.

35. Ford, Worthington Chauncey. "Public Records in Our Dependencies." *Annual Report of the American Historical Association* (1904): 131-47.

36. Ibid., 147.

37. Ibid., 134.

38. Ibid., 140-141.

39. Robertson, James Alexander. "Notes on the Archives of the Philippines." *Annual Report of the American Historical Association* (1910): 421-26.10n 1904 and 190101, RG 350, NACes.

40. Ford, 133.

41. Robertson, 423.

42. Ibid.

43. Ibid., 425.

44. Robertson to Governor-General, May 10, 1912, file 702, RG 350, NACP.

45. Ibid.

46. Yriarte to Minturn, May 4, 1912, file 702, RG 350, NACP. In the same file as Yriarte's memo is another, unfortunately unsigned. Unlike Yriarte, it concurred with Robertson's views and noted both the historical and administrative value of the records: "Among the

documents now in Spain there are, I understand, important papers affecting proprietary rights of citizens and residents of the Philippine Islands. Such documents have only a historical value to the Spanish Government and people but would in a large number of cases be of immense practical value to the Government and people of the Philippine Islands and for this reason should, if it can, be obtained. [...] The question whether such documents, if obtained, should go to enrich the Philippine Library or should go to complete the Division of Archives of the Executive Bureau is a matter that may be decided later."

47. Robertson to Governor-General, May 10, 1912, file 702, RG 350, NACP.

48. McIntyre to Woodson, Mar. 31, 1913, file 702, RG 350, NACP. See also Woodson to McIntyre, Apr. 2, 1913, file 702, RG 350, NACP. For further criticism of Roberton's request, see also Knox to Oliver, Aug. 15, 1912, file 702, RG 350, NACP.

49. McIntyre to Governor-General, Apr. 11, 1913, file 702, RG 350, NACP. McIntyre's letter continues: "Without going into the question as to whether we are entitled to these documents under the terms of the Treaty of Paris, it seems to me that if such right existed it should have been exercised long ago and that unless we can present a real active necessity for these documents in the administration of affairs of the Philippine Islands we could only present a poor case which would receive no consideration."

50. John R.M. Taylor Papers, Division of Manuscripts, Library of Congress (LOC).

51. Constantino, introduction to *The Philippine Insurrection against the United States*, x-xi; and John T. Farrell, "An Abandoned Approach to Philippine History: John R.M. Taylor and the Philippine Insurrection Records," *Catholic History Review* 39, no.4 (Jan. 1954): 385-407.

52. Constantino, Renato. Introduction to *The Philippine Insurrection against the United States: A Compilation of Documents with Notes and Introduction,* edited by John R.M. Taylor, ix-xii. Pasig City: Eugenio Lopez Foundation, 1971.

53. "Additional Appendices to the Annual Report of Major General Arthur MacArthur, Military Governor of the Philippine Islands, 1900," file 1239, RG 350, NACP. MacArthur's report continues, noting that: "The completion of the work of classification and translation of the more important documents will necessitate the continuance of this office for a considerable period."

54. Taylor to Dietrich, 1902, outgoing letters, RG 350, NACP. Taylor goes on to explain that though he had not conducted extensive research into the "personal records" of the people profiled in his report, "it can be said generally that almost without exception they are Tagalogs and have been associated with uprisings against Spain."

55. Taylor to Edwards, May 1, 1906, outgoing letters, RG 350, NACP.

56. Bureau of Insular Affairs Chief Clarence Ransom Edwards explained this situation to Secretary of the Interior Dean C. Worcester, in his response to a request for information to be derived from the captured records. Edwards to Worcester, Nov. 19, 1908, outgoing letters, RG 350, NACP.

57. Taylor to Edwards, Aug. 6, 1903, outgoing letters, RG 350, NACP; Edwards to Taft, Aug. 6, 1903, outgoing letters, RG 350, NACP. As to be expected, the transfer of records was sometimes achieved without incident, especially after major hostilities had subsided; see, for example, McIntyre to Smith, Dec. 22, 1908, outgoing letters, RG 350, NACP.

58. Edwards to Taft, May 23, 1903, outgoing letters, RG 350, NACP; in this letter from Edwards notes that Taylor knows of the existence of Tagalog dictionaries among the friars, as one was found among the captured records of Emilio Aguinaldo.

59. Edwards to Wright, Jan. 9, 1904, outgoing letters, RG 350, NACP; Edwards to Root, July 29, 1903, outgoing letters, RG 350, NACP.

60. Bureau of Insular Affairs memo, Apr. 8, 1905, outgoing letters, RG 350, NACP; Scofield to Edwards, June 21, 1906, outgoing letters, RG 350, NACP; McIntyre to Fergusson, Sept. 3, 1907, outgoing letters, RG 350, NACP; McIntyre memo, Oct. 7, 1907, outgoing letters, RG 350, NACP.

61. McIntyre to LeRoy, Mar. 13, 1908, outgoing letters, RG 350, NACP.

62. Taft to McIntyre, Aug. 16, 1906, Clarence Ransom Edwards Papers, Massachusetts Historical Society (MHS). See also McIntyre to Taft, July 27, 1906, outgoing letters, RG 350, NACP. As Secretary of War with a looming presidential primary campaign, however, Taft was pressed for time and revisions to Taylor's introduction unsurprisingly languished; see Edwards to Putnam, Jan. 9, 1907, outgoing letters, RG 350, NACP.

63. Taylor to Edwards, Aug. 23, 1906. Edwards Papers, MHS.

64. McIntyre to LeRoy, Dec. 28, 1908, outgoing letters, RG 350, NACP; McIntyre to Forbes, Sept. 17, 1909, outgoing letters, RG 350, NACP; Edwards to Wright, Jan. 10, 1909, outgoing letters, RG 350, NACP.

65. LeRoy to Robertson, Jan. 11, 1909, box 5, James A. Robertson Papers, LOC.

66. Edwards to Wright, Jan. 10, 1909, outgoing letters, RG 350, NACP.

67. "Exhibit 9: Original notes for the decree establishing the Provisional Government of the Philippines, May 24, 1898," in *The Philippine Insurrection against the United States,* ed. John R.M. Taylor (Pasay City, 1971), 3:34-5.

68. Rifles, "Exhibit 16, June 3, 1898," in ibid., 3:44; "the amount of money," "Exhibit 49, July 2, 1898," in ibid., 3:152; "all the property," "Exhibit 123, Aug. 9, 1898," in ibid., 3:210. See also "Exhibit 124, Aug. 11, 1898," in ibid., 3:211-2.

69. "Exhibit 1315, Dionisio Papa to Rufo Oyos, May 19, 1900," in ibid., 5:625. During this period, Governor and General Leandro Fullon ordered: "1. Any meeting or assembly of a popular character, held at the instance of the Officers of the United States, for the purpose of recognizing the liberty and independence of the towns of this province, is absolutely forbidden. 2. The person arranging such meeting shall be shot at once without trial or court martial, unless forced to do so by force majeure. 3. Any Filipino filling any office in the name of the United States shall be considered a traitor to his country, and in addition to the penalties imposed by the Penal Code of Spain, provisionally in force, all his property shall be confiscated, and if this should not be possible, the authorities of the Philippine Republic shall endeavor to *** (remainder of sentence unintelligible)." "Exhibit 1293, July 11, 1900," in ibid., 5:595. See also "Exhibit 1301, Oct. 1, 1900," in ibid., 5:603-4.

70. "Exhibit 26, June 11, 1898," in ibid., 3:99.

71. "Exhibit 303, Nov. 30, 1898," in ibid., 3:416-7.

72. Ibid. Article 1 of this decree states: "Instruments or contracts which may have as an object the creation, transfer, modification or extinction of real rights over landed property situated in the territory of the Philippine Islands, and leases of the same property, provided that the latter may prejudice a third party, must set forth in a public instrument, which shall be executed before an official of this Government empowered to certify to documents."

73. "Exhibit 952, Feb. 27, 1899," in ibid., 4:736-45. Later, the Philippine Commission's Act No. 496, also known as the Land Registration Act, approximated the Office of the Secretary of Agriculture, Industry and Commerce's regulations.

74. "Exhibit 36, June 20, 1898," in ibid., 3:120. These instructions state, in part: "Rule 25. The same Commissioner [of Justice] shall keep three books; one in which he shall enter the births, in chronological order, specifying the name of the new-born, the place and day of birth, the names, surnames, and residence of the parents of the same, and lastly, the name, surname and residence of the God-father, who shall sign the entry as witness with the Chief and the aforesaid Commissioner. Rule 26. He shall keep another book in which he shall enter the deaths, giving the name, surname, profession, conjugal conditions and residence of the deceased, the names, surnames and residence of the parents of the same, and the disease and cause of death. The entry shall be signed by the Chief and the Commissioner, together with a witness who shall be a member of the family or a

neighbor of the deceased. Rule 27. In the third book marriage contracts shall be entered, after conforming to the following requisites: The contracting parties shall sign a paper stating to the Chief of the town that by mutual consent they have agreed to marry, and requesting that he proceed to enter said contract in the public registry. If the contracting parties be under twenty-three years of age, their respective fathers shall subscribe the paper with them; in the absence of these, the mothers, and lacking both of these, the elder brothers, who shall have completed twenty-one years [...]."

75. "Exhibit 858, Apr. 10, 1899," in ibid., 4:620.

76. "Exhibit 431, Oct. 8, 1898," in ibid., 3:561.

77. The remainder of the draft reads: "and in these models it shall be endeavored to do away with entirely the discredited Spanish method observed heretofore in treating with the disdained and unfortunate Gobernadorcillos and Municipal Captains, now Local Chiefs, it depending on the judgment of the writer, be it clear and upright or otherwise, whether the form be dignified and decorous or disrespectful and offensive, and which, if the latter, will only cause a dislike for the service and indifference on the part of the person called upon to do anything, which in turn causes controversies and divisions favorable to the enemy, that a clever government with good foresight should avoid through rules and measures that aim at attaining that cohesion of all its citizens so necessary at a time of Independence." "Bases of a Resolution for the Regulation of Official Communications Directed to the Local Authorities, Exhibit 348, [1899?]," in ibid., 3:451.

78. "Exhibit 47, June 27, 1898," in ibid., 3:147. Approximately two months later, "Statement of the Personnel Composing the Revolutionary Government of the Philippines" was circulated, providing greater detail to the June 27 instructions: "Exhibit 260, Sept. 26, 1898," in ibid., 3:364-68.

79. A more detailed description of the charge of the Department of the Treasury was offered later that summer. See "Exhibit 124, Aug. 11, 1898," in ibid., 3:211-12. Per a statement issued on September 26, 1898, the departments of Fomento and Justice were added to the central government, and administrative responsibilities somewhat redistributed. See "Exhibit 261, Sept. 26, 1898," in ibid., 3:368-70. At a later date, the Department of Agriculture, Industry and Commerce was charged with the regulation of "proprietary rights of manufacturing and commercial marks," which, under the Americans, would fall to the Division of Archives, Copyrights and Trademarks. See "Exhibit 509, Jan. 20, 1899," in ibid., 3:666-67.

80. "Exhibit 465, Oct. 26, 1898," in ibid., 3:608-10.

81. Inspectors were sent to "carefully examine the papers and books kept in each presidente's office and see if they conform to the requirements of our decrees, and especially in the case of the account books; compare also very carefully the receipts with the expenditures and if you should not any defalcation of malversation or other illegal acts, you will institute the proper proceedings and suspend the guilty persons, appointing temporary substitutes for them and calling new election for officials who are to take the places of the defaulters, without prejudice to the instructions requested of this Department [of the Interior.]" "Exhibit 470, Nov. 23, 1898," in ibid., 3:614-5. The guidelines for the inspection reports were included in several documents: "Exhibit 471, [Nov. 23, 1898?]," in ibid., 3:615-17; "Exhibit 474, Dec. 20, 1898," in ibid., 3:620-21; "Exhibit 475, [Dec. 1898]," in ibid., 3:621-22.

82. "Exhibit 47, June 27, 1898," in ibid., 3:148. The rather involved protocol required: "The assistants in the bureaus shall draw up a record of each case, to which they will add the documents which may be necessary, requesting these of the interested parties or of the other offices, through official letters, which the directors or provincial and popular chiefs shall sign. When all the data and necessary documents are attached to the record, the assistant shall make an abstract, specifying clearly the object of the business and the evidence which appears pro and con in the same. With this abstract it shall be forwarded to the official in charge, who will countersign it, or append a memorandum of the changes and observations which he may make, and at the end state his opinion upon the decision to be adopted, forwarding the record at once to the director. The latter shall examine the record and confer with the Secretary so as to prepare the decision in the form of a decree or order, which the latter shall submit for the approval and signature of the President of the Government, if no prior consultation with Congress be necessary. The provincial and popular offices shall observe similar formalities."

83. "Exhibit 508, Nov. 29, 1898," in ibid., 3:664.

84. "Exhibit 655, May 8, 1899," in ibid., 4:98. The maintenance of archives within government departments may have been the practice in some departments, before it was mandated for all departments; a memorandum to the Secretary of the Interior, dated March 17, 1899, indicates the one of the special powers of the department was "To order that in this officer there be kept a registry book wherein entry shall be made of all papers that come in and go out of the same; and that an archive be formed of all the papers (expedients) relating to questions finally settled." "Exhibit 792, Mar. 17, 1899," in ibid., 4:517. The reasoning that prompted this decentralization may be gleaned from documents the detail the extensive and complicated nature of the records each department was charged to generate. See, for example, the instructions and reports from the Bureau of Information within the Department of Foreign Affairs and the Treasury Department: "Exhibit 732,

July 26, 1899," in ibid., 4:231-32; and "Exhibit 751, Feb. 12, 1899," in ibid., 4:305-8.

85. "Exhibit 886, May 25, 1899," in ibid., 4:649.

86. Constantino, introduction to *The Philippine Insurrection against the United States*, ix.

87. Forbes to Storey, Jan. 3, 1905, Moorfield Storey Papers, LOC.

88. Schurz to Adams, Oct. 25, 1900, Charles Francis Adams II Papers, MHS. Schurz wrote more specifically: "I have laboriously and carefully studied what has happened in all its details and bearings, and that study has profoundly convinced me that the story of our "criminal aggression" upon the Philippines is a story of deceit, false presence, brutal treachery to friends, unconstitutional assumption of power, downright betrayal of the fundamental principles of our democracy, wanton sacrifice of our soldiers in a wicked war, cruel slaughter of tens of thousands of innocent people, and that of horrible blood,– guiltless, without parallel in the history of republics; and that such a policy is bound to bring upon this republic evils infinitely more disgraceful and disastrous in their effects than anything that has been predicted as likely to result from Mr. McKinley's defeat."

89. Ingalsbe to Atkinson, Oct. 10, 1900, Edward Atkinson Papers, MHS; Atkinson to Osborne, July 3, 1900, Atkinson Papers, MHS; White to Adams, Apr. 26, 1906, Adams Papers, MHS.

90. Charles H. Parkhurst, *The Philippine Islands: Their Permanent Tenure a Folly and a Crime: A Sermon Preached by Reverend Charles H. Parkhurst at the Madison Square Presbyterian Church, New York, November 24, 1898* (New York, 1898), 13.

91. Taft to Hollister, Dec. 1, 1900, reel 31, Taft Papers, LOC. Regarding anti-imperialists and civil service reform, see Taft to Foulke, May 18, 1901, reel 32, Taft Papers, LOC. Erving Winslow's conviction, early stated, that the Anti-Imperialist League be a single-issue organization seems to have won the day, Winslow to Atkinson, June 23, 1898, Atkinson Papers, MHS.

92. Ida B. Wells, *Southern Horrors and Other Writings: The Anti-Lynching Campaign of Ida B. Well, 1892-1900*, ed. Jacqueline Jones Royster (Boston: Bedford/St. Martins, 1997); Jacqueline Goldsby, *A Spectacular Secret: Lynching in American Life and Literature* (Chicago: University of Chicago Press, 2006), especially chapter 2, "Writing "Dynamitically": Ida B. Wells." The Anti-Imperialist League used this same model in its pamphlet "Marked Severities." Sending a copy to a colleague, Charles Francis Adams noted that every fact "was carefully verified from official documents. Tortures was of every day occurrence; ravishing, not infrequent;–murders too common to specify." Adams to Hull, Jan. 10, 1906, Adams Papers, MHS.

93. See, for example, Minutes of the Executive Committee of the New England Anti-Imperialist League, Dec. 24, 1902, vol. 2, Erving Winslow Papers, Special Collections Library, University of Michigan (Michigan); Atkinson to Taussig, Apr. 11, 1899, Atkinson Papers, MHS.

94. "Exhibit 916, [Sept. 1899]," in *Philippine Insurrection against the United States*, ed. Taylor, 4:697.

95. Andrew Carnegie, "Should the United States Expand?," in *Republic or Empire? The Philippine Question*, 89-99. Carnegie observed: "The entrance of the United States into the zone of constant dread of war is even more to be feared than the danger of actual war itself, except so far as the latter involve direct sacrifice of human life. On the other hand, lack of steady employment through seasons of panic caused by alarm of war also claims its victims, sometimes in the course of years even exceeding in number those who fall in battle. There can be no genuine prosperity in a country which is kept in constant apprehension of war," 96-97.

96. Schurz to Adams, Feb. 8, 1903, Adams Papers, MHS.

97. Atkinson to Mason, May 1, 1902, Atkinson Papers, MHS. See also, Atkinson to Gilman, Nov. 7, 1898, for Atkinson's economic argument against slavery as it related to the annexation of Texas, Atkinson Papers, MHS.

98. Hoar to Atkinson, Nov. 21, 1899, Atkinson Papers, MHS; Hoar to Adams, Nov. 29, 1898, Adams Papers, MHS.

99. Ibid.

100. Samuel Gompers, "Imperialism: Dangers and Wrongs," in *Republic or Empire? The Philippine Question* (Chicago: The Independence Company, 1899), 209-11. Gompers wrote: "When innocent men can be shot down on the public highway as they were in Lattimer, PA, and Virden, Ill., men of our own flesh and blood, men who help to make this homogenous nation great, because they dare to ask for more humane conditions at the hands of the moneyed class of our country, how much more difficult will it be to arouse any sympathy, and secure relief for the poor semi-savages in the Philippines, must less indignation at any crime against their inherent and natural rights to life, liberty, and the pursuit of happiness" (211).

101. John Daniel, "The Effect of Annexation of the Philippines on American Labor," in *Republic or Empire? The Philippine Question*, 367-425; Anti-Imperialist League, *Philippine Independence: Discussion of Hon. W.H. Taft's Letter, March 16, 1905* (Boston: Anti-Imperialist League, 1905), 16.

102. Nell Irvin Painter, *Standing at Armageddon: A Grassroots History of the Progressive Era* (New York: W.W. Norton, 2008), 259.

103. Adams to Lodge, Sept. 30, 1902, Adams Papers, MHS.

104. Adams to Schurman, Aug. 4, 1902, Adams Papers, MHS. In this letter, Adams assessed Roosevelt's proclamation of amnesty "was statesmanlike." For more on Adams's positive view of Roosevelt's proclamation, see also Adams to Welsh, Aug. 4, 1902, Adams Papers, MHS.

105. For a resonant scholarly argument, see Gary Wills, *Lincoln at Gettysburg: The Words That Remade America* (New York: Simon and Schuster, 1993).

106. "You unquestionably hold fresh in memory the disastrous results of the experiment at 'reconstruction' we attempted in the case of the Confederate States during the administration of Andrew Jackson. We must all be anxious that there should be no repetition of the experience in the case of the Philippines; and the only way, we believe, to avoid a repetition is to proceed in some well-considered way, on a basis of real knowledge of conditions in the Archipelago." Adams to Cooper, June 28, 1902, Adams Papers, MHS. On national character, see Adams to Norton, Apr. 15, 1902, box 1, Herbert Welsh Papers, Michigan; on military accountability, see Adams to Welsh, July 10, 1902, box 1, Welsh Papers, Michigan; Adams to Willis, Aug. 16, 1902, Adams Papers, MHS; Adams to Willis, Oct. 30, 1902, Adams Papers, MHS.

107. George Frisbie Hoar, *Speech of Honorable George Frisbie Hoar, of Massachusetts, in the Senate of the United States, May 22, 1902* (Washington: Government Printing Office, 1902), 3. Citing fellow senators, Hoar continued his critique: "I see that my enthusiastic friend from North Carolina seeks to break the force of these revelations [of torture] by saying that they are only what some Americans are wont to do at home. It is benevolent assimilation all over again. It is just what the junior senator from Indiana predicted. He thought we should conduct affairs in the Philippines Islands so admirably that we should pattern our domestic administration on that model. But did I understand that the senator from North Carolina proposes, if his charge against the Democrats there is true, to make North Carolina a howling wilderness, or to burn populous towns of 10,000 people, to get the people of North Carolina into reconcentration camps, and to slay every male child over ten years old?" 29.

108. Carnegie to Adams, Feb. 5, 1901, Adams Papers, MHS.

109. Adams wrote: "So far as politics and the development of results in this country are concerned, I am well satisfied no amount of work on our part would accomplish much under existing conditions. The country is thoroughly apathetic. It is prosperous, growing

rapidly, making money fast. Under these circumstances, it does not wish to bother itself over moral, or other, questions, and it gives languid ear to those who insist upon bothering it. A clear and striking case in point is that of these labor troubles, and this tendency to lynching. Both are regarded in an apathetic sort of way, as if the general consciousness was that, somehow or other, they would in good time cure themselves." Adams to Welsh, July 21, 1903, box 1, Welsh Papers, Michigan. See also Adams to Carnegie, Feb. 10, 1903, Adams Papers, MHS. With regard to moral imperatives, David Starr Jordan provided an interesting counterpoint several years earlier: "If it were possible to exterminate the Filipinos as we have destroyed the Indians, replacing their institutions and their people by ours, the political objections to annexation would, in the main, disappear whatever might be said of the moral ones. For our treatment of the Indians, there is, in general, no moral justification. There is a good political excuse in this—that we could and did use their land in a better way than was possible to them. We have no such excuse in Luzon; we cannot use the land except as we can use the lives of the people." David Starr Jordan, *The Question of the Philippines* (Palo Alto, CA: Graduate Club, 1899), 26.

110. Charles Morris, *The War with Spain* (Philadelphia: J.B. Lippincott, 1899), 383. Charles Francis Adams had his doubt about the unifying work of war: "Every nation which has undertaken to colonize in Asia, or the tropics, has had first to shot-gun the inferior race into submission, then flog them into obedience. I fancy we have a somewhat similar experience before us; and when confronted with that experience, I imagine our people may revise conclusions they are now quick to reach." Adams to Hoar, Dec. 20, 1898, George Frisbie Hoar Papers, MHS.

111. Storey to Winslow, Dec. 20, 1916, box 1, Winslow Papers, Michigan; Storey to Winslow, Oct. 14, 1917, box1, Winslow Papers, Michigan; Storey to Winslow, Apr. 11, 1919, box 1, Winslow Papers, Michigan.

112. Clement to Winslow, Aug. 11, 1917, box 1, Winslow Papers, Michigan. Clement continued: "Persevere we must, on all proper occasions, in insisting on independence for the Philippines,–which indeed, thanks to the faithful and sagacious and gracious support of President Wilson, we have written in solemn words into laws enacted by Congress. But pertinacity in pressing our special and particular purpose with the country embarking on a new departure perfectly stupendous in its implications, as to our committals in world politics, amounts, under the circumstances, to what our enemies would call, impertinence!"

113. Storey to Winslow, Mar. 14, 1918, box 1, Winslow Papers, Michigan. See also Perry to Winslow, Apr. 9, 1918, box 1, Winslow Papers, Michigan.

114. Minutes of the Executive Committee of the Anti-Imperialist League, Jan. 3, 1918, vol. 5, Winslow Papers, Michigan; Jordan to Winslow, July 21, 1917, Erving Winslow

Papers, MHS.

115. Hoar to Storey, Mar. 6, 1899, Storey Papers, LOC. Hoar continued: "The masses of the people, of both parties, think it is very strong evidence that a proposition is wrong when such gentlemen believe in it. I have myself pitched into them a good deal, and at the same time have had a very kindly side toward them, as I had toward the old Garrison abolitionists in their day. But their utterances seem not like those of a man desires to make converts or to accomplish results, but when they have borne their own testimony against what they think wrong, they seem not only contented to remain in the minority, but rather to like and prefer it."

116. Lovering to Adams, May 19, 1899, Adams Papers, MHS. What Lovering confided to Adams, Hoar wrote directly to Atkinson: "You are a good man and I like you, and the hard things that I have ever had occasion to say about you I have always said to you and have stood up for you pretty stoutly in many companies of your critics. But you are wrong from the top of your head to the sole of your foot, not in principle, still less in purpose, but in your utter incapacity to understand the point of you of other men and your inability to see that men who are looking at the other side of the shield may be as honest, as desirous for the public good and often quite as intelligent as yourself." Hoar to Atkinson, Jan. 21, 1901, Atkinson Papers, MHS.

117. W. Cameron Forbes journal, June 10, 1906, W. Cameron Forbes Journals, MHS. Forbes' opposition to anti-imperialist impulses in the United States is well-documented in his journals; see, for example: "I wonder if the fool-killer has gone out of business in the United States. Every one he has spared seems to have a new plan of disposing of the Philippines, each one sillier than the last; and the wild-eyed enthusiasts seem to suggest many alternatives, always ignoring the sane and simple one, so easily to hand, of sitting tight and doing nothing but what we are doing. That very reasonable solution seems to have escaped nine-tenths of those whose views penetrate the cables and reach us." Forbes journal, Sept. 28, 1907, Forbes Journals, MHS; and "The only things on my desk to be taken up are the paper relating to representation by Irving Winslow and the Anti-Imperialist League that I take to be libellous on me and that I may go after in the courts at home if I have a good show of winning, as I want to punish one or two scoundrels [...]." Forbes journal, July 23, 1911, Forbes Journals, MHS.

118. LeRoy to Garrison, Jan. 19, 1904, letterbook, James Alfred LeRoy Papers, Bentley Historical Library, University of Michigan (BHL); for other expressions of LeRoy's opposition to United States colonial policy and aversion to anti-imperialists, see LeRoy to Doherty, Dec. 21, 19004, letterbook, LeRoy Papers, BHL; Leroy to Park, Sept. 15, 1904, letterbook, LeRoy Papers, BHL.

119. Hoar to Lodge, Oct. 10, 1903, Henry Cabot Lodge Papers, MHS. Hoar's view is made further apparent in his letters to former Massachusetts Governor George S. Boutwell. Shortly after the conclusion of the Spanish-American War, he wrote: "We have been somewhat unfortunate in the fact that the gentlemen who have come to the front in the matter of opposing the treaty or acquisition of foreign territory are men who have been, in the judgment of the people, in the wrong almost always in the past, and are regarded not only as unsafe, but as very absurd leaders." Hoar to Boutwell, Dec. 31, 1898, Hoar Papers, MHS; and reflecting back on the re-election of McKinley, which Hoar had supported, he wrote: "President Harrison, Mr. Reed, Senator Edmunds, President Schurman, President Eliot, President Hadley and hosts of other men eminent for integrity, ability and large public influence took the same position that I did. If it had been taken by all the Anti-Imperialists we should have defeated Imperialism, and the position of the little company in Boston would not have injured—as it did—the cause of Anti-Imperialism by making it utterly ridiculous." Hoar to Boutwell, July 20, 1904, Hoar Papers, MHS. Writing to Adams about the matter or torture in the Philippines, Hoar managed to include an assessment of Moorfield Storey: "He is an able lawyer, and has great capacity for public usefulness. But he seems to me to be a monomaniac on political questions. When I talk with him and any political matter about which he is deeply interested comes up, his countenance changes and a look comes over it which I have frequently seen come over the countenance of a man, otherwise sane, but has insane delusions. He seems to be absolutely incapable of believing that a man can differ from him without being a scoundrel. [...] The result of this trait in Storey is that his very able arguments on public questions lose much of their weight from the fact that they are published under his name. It is very unfortunate for the man, and unfortunate for the public when the people are prejudiced against good and strong arguments because of their dislike of the mental quality of the author." Hoar to Adams, Sept. 29, 1902, Hoar Papers, MHS.

120. Quezon to Willis, Aug. 7, 1914, reel 5, Manuel Luis Quezon Papers, BHL; see also Aug. 19, 1914, reel 5, Quezon Papers, BHL. Though Quezon and Winslow frequently disagreed (Quezon to Winslow, Aug. 7, 1914, Aug. 17, 1914, Sept. 16, 1914, Oct. 3, 1914; Winslow to Quezon, Aug. 15, 1914, Sept. 17, 1914) about United States-Philippine politics, they did maintain regular correspondence throughout the efforts to pass the Jones Bill. In 1916, Quezon graciously thanked Winslow, despite the latter's many, animated criticisms: "I wish to renew the expressions of my profound appreciation for the noble work done by the Anti-Imperialist League in favor of Philippine independence. My people owe the League an eternal gratitude. I am sure that we never would have secured as much as we have, had it not been for the untiring campaign of the League. We have not, as yet, reached the goal, but I have no doubt that you will and I am confident that the League will, continue the fight until complete victory is won." Quezon to Winslow, Aug. 21,

1916, reel 7, Quezon Papers, BHL.

121. Quezon to Storey, June 8, 1919, reel 9, Quezon Papers, BHL.

122. See, for example, the criticism from the editorial director of the *American Union against Militarism*: "It has always been a source of dissatisfaction to me that the Anti-Imperialist League has stayed in Boston and maintained what, rightly or wrongly, have always seemed to me to be "genteel" methods of propaganda. Boston, like Oxford, is the home of lost causes, whereas Washington is the home of big crass middle class movements which unaccountably muddle through to success." Hallinan to Brooks, Dec. 21, 1916, box 2, Winslow Papers, Michigan.

123. Beyond serving the political needs of that particular moment, the work of the Anti-Imperialist League would maintain some level of influence into the twentieth century. By the last quarter of the twentieth century, as the American war in Vietnam escalated, the United States' involvement in the Philippines and the Anti-Imperialist's critique of that involvement enjoyed a renewed currency. In other words, activists, critics and historians found that the questions that the Anti-Imperialist League raised in 1899 resonated. While this process of "remembering" a "forgotten" war was prompted by the political needs of that moment. See, for example, Daniel Schirmer, *Republic or Empire: American Resistance to the Philippine War* (Cambridge, MA: Schenkman Publishing, 1972).

124. Minutes of the Executive Committee of the New England Anti-Imperialist League, May 2, 1901 Vol. 1, Winslow Papers, Michigan.

125. Winslow to Quezon, July 31, 1912, reel 3, Quezon Papers, BHL. For his part, Quezon doubted that Blount's omission indicated a sinister move, Quezon to Winslow, July 31, 1912, reel 3, Quezon Papers, BHL.

126. By contrast, Schurz noted that he himself was "always considered, or at least called, a radical extremist." Schurz to Adams, May 7, 1902, box 2, Welsh Papers, Michigan.

127. Atkinson to Gage, Apr. 22, 1899, Atkinson Papers, MHS. Both Erving Winslow and Winslow Warren of the Anti-Imperialist League were critical of Atkinson's actions, and the organization went so far as to publicly differentiate Atkinson's personal actions from those of the league, Warren to Atkinson, May 5, 1899, Atkinson Papers, MHS. In turn, Atkinson wrote to Winslow: "It may embarrass you to have my name remain as a Vice-President of the League. You may therefore remove it if you see fit, and if I have occasion hereafter to communication with you or the Executive Committee in advising any course in which the Executive Committee may differ, I will be careful to mark my letters "Private" or "Not for publication," Atkinson Papers, MHS.

128. Vaille to Smith, Sept. 24, 1900, entry 5, box 274, RG 350, NACP; General Order 24 from the Bureau of Posts of the Philippine Islands, Sept. 26, 1903, entry 5, box 274, RG 350, NACP; Edwards to MacCarthy, May 24, 1900, outgoing letters, RG 350, NACP. In the first decade of rule, the colonial administration's attention to mail does not seem to have waned, though the war had officially concluded. While in 1900, Director-General of Posts F.W. Vaille had contended that "censorship shall be resorted to only in case of absolute necessity," by 1909, the censorship of mail had grown to be quite ambitious; General Order 1, Jan. 8, 1909, from the Bureau of Posts of the Philippine Islands read: "Every obscene, lewd, lascivious, indecent, filthy book, pamphlet, picture, paper, letter, writing, print or publication, and every publication of an indecent character, and every article or thing designed or intended for the prevention of conception or the procuring of an abortion, and every article or thing intended for or adapted to any indecent or immoral use, and every written or printed card, letter, circular, book, pamphlet, advertisement, or notice of any kind giving information, directly or indirectly, where or how or of whom or by what means any of all the hereinbefore mentioned matters, articles or things may be obtained or made, and any mail matter containing any filthy, foul, or indecent article, device, or substance, whether sealed as first-class matter or not, shall not be conveyed in the mails or delivered from any post office nor by any letter carrier, and shall be withdrawn from the mails and forwarded to the Dead Letter Office of this Bureau for destruction. All matter otherwise mailable by law upon which may be written or printed or otherwise impressed or apparent, any delineations, epithets, terms, or language of an indecent, lewd, obsence, filthy, libelous, scurrilous, defamatory or threatening character, or calculated by the terms or manner or style of display and obviously intended to reflect injuriously upon the character or conduct of another, shall not be conveyed in the mail or delivered from any post office nor by any letter carrier, and shall be withdrawn from the mails and forwarded to the Dead Letter Office of this Bureau for destruction." Entry 5, box 274, RG 350, NACP.

129. Mercer to Welsh, Dec. 31, 1901, box 1, Welsh Papers, Michigan; Peypoch to Sniffen, Nov. 6, 1902, box 1, Welsh Papers, Michigan; Wilby to Welsh, Nov. 5, 1900, box 2, Welsh Papers, Michigan; Adams to Schurz, Dec. 15, 1902, Adams Papers, MHS; Atkinson to Jennings, Feb. 25, 1902, Atkinson Papers, MHS; Atkinson to Hoar, Feb. 24, 1899, Atkinson Papers, MHS. This is not to suggest that the suppression of information was an altogether successful endeavor, as the letters home from American soldiers and the legacy of the so-called "seditious Tagalog playwrights" attest. See for example, Starr to Lawton, Aug. 2, 1899: "General Lawton requests that in the future you will not discuss any official matter of any nature whatsoever with any person or persons, either in this office or out of it, except in the proper transaction of official business. This request is rendered necessary by reason of allegations made by the Department Commander that

many official matters have become known to newspaper correspondents and others, to the detriment of the service, through remarks made by the members of the Staff of this Division," Edwards Papers, MHS.

130. Atkinson to Udell, May 18, 1899, Atkinson Papers, MHS.

131. Atkinson to U.S. Attorney General, May 5, 1899, Atkinson Papers, MHS; Atkinson to Carnegie, May 5, 1899, Atkinson Papers, MHS.

132. Baird to Atkinson, May 3, 1899, Atkinson Papers, MHS; Winslow, May 8, 1899, Atkinson Papers, MHS.

133. Firth to Atkinson, June 12, 1899, Atkinson Papers, MHS. The two public libraries referred to here are the Merrimac Public Library and the Whitefield Public Library, McConnell to Atkinson, Aug. 8, 1899, Wright to Atkinson, Oct. 18, 1899, Atkinson Papers, MHS.

134. Atkinson to Bowditch, May 4, 1899, Atkinson Papers, MHS.

135. Warren to Atkinson, May 3, 1899, Atkinson Papers, MHS.

136. Writing to Herbert Welsh, Sniffen reported: "I think I also sent you a clipping telling you of the formation of a Society in Boston, Thursday of this week, for the purpose of bringing to light information regarding the Philippines that is now buried in varous reports, letters and documents that are on file in the Government's depositories. The people who are at the head of this movement have heretofore been 'on the fence.'" Sniffen to Welsh, Dec. 15, 1900, box 2, Welsh Papers, Michigan. Two days later, Sniffed continued: "The newly formed 'Philippine Information Society' is preparing to rehash the facts that have already been published, for the most part, by the Anti-Imperialists. Of course, they aim for some new material, but it will practically amount to using the Anti-Imperialist statements without the association of the League's name. Mrs. Glendomar [?] Evans who is the moving spirit in the enterprise said to me, with a great deal of force, that their organization can get many good people to read information quite readily, who would be scared off by any statement coming from the Anti-Imperialist League; that the name seems to be a 'bugaboo.' The general effect produced on these people is to arouse their interest and convert them unconsciously into the most rabid anti-imperialists, although they would hardly admit it. In some respects the new movement is amusing. The promoters do not care in any way to be associated with those who have all along borne the brunt of the battle, on account of existing prejudices. Some of these good people are inclined to believe that President McKinley is ignorant of the true conditions in the Philippines, that his information was derived second hand, etc." Sniffen to Welsh, Dec. 17, 1900, box 2, Welsh Papers, Michigan.

137. Porter to Schurman, Feb. 24, 1900, Jacob Gould Schurman Papers, Division of Rare and Manuscript Collections, Cornell University (RMC); Porter to Schurman, Oct. 27, 1900, correspondence, Schurman papers, RMC.

138. Howells to Schurman, Jan. 27, 1902, correspondence, Schurman papers, RMC.

139. Scott to Schurman, Apr. 11, 1902, correspondence, Schurman papers, RMC.

140. Sixto Lopez to Schurman, May 20, 1902, correspondence, Schurman papers, RMC.

141. Taft to Seymour, Mar. 16, 1903, reel 38, Taft Papers, LOC. When working together on the first Philippine Commission, Dean Worcester's writing did little to conceal his dislike for Schurman: "He has seriously injured his standing with the authorities at Washington, and I fancy his career as a diplomat will be decidedly rocket-like. He soared rapidly, but has begun to come down now. It would be like him to go home and try to become the apostle of the "antis." Well, we shall see." Michigan, Worcester, vol. 16. See also, Worcester, July 5, 1899: "Schurman announced yesterday that he must leave here by July 1st, or thereabouts! [...] Every one was glad to hear he meant to go so soon, and no one asked him why he had changed his mind. He probably sees that he cannot rule the roost here, and wants to get home and try to influence the President. If he had not send [sic] that telegram I should be more or less afraid of him, but as it is I fear his career as a diplomat will not be prolonged!" Vol. 16, Dean Worcester Papers, Michigan.

142. Jordan, 8. See Taft to Hoyt, Nov. 3, 1900: "I have not received from you Root's speech or Richards [sic] speech, but General Corbis sent me a copy of Root's speech and I think it is the best presentation possible. It is a very able document and shows the flimsy character of the alleged facts upon which most of the anti-imperialist argument proceeds." Edwards Papers, MHS.

143. "But the largest and most influential class from which the administration derives its information is that of the American officeholder whose names are truly legion. These men are naturally in full accord with the policies of the administration to whom they owe their positions. They wish to continue to hold their jobs, and it is absurd to support that they will ever give public utterance to opinion not in accord with those held by the powers that be. Many of them have no sympathy for the poor Filipinos, and some, at least, despise them and take no pains to disguise the fact." William A. Jones, *Misgovernment in the Philippines and Cost to the United States of American Occupation: Speech of Hon. William A. Jones of Virginia in the House of Representatives, January 28, 1913* (Washington: Government Printing Office, 1913), 23.

144. Charles Francis Adams, Carl Schurz, Edwin Burritt Smith, Herbert Welsh, and Andrew Carnegie composed the committee. See their report, July 23, 1902, reel 319,

Taft Papers, LOC. The committee was formed, in Adams's words, for the purpose "of taking whatever steps might be necessary to effect a full disclosure of facts connected with processes and executions in the course of military operations in the Philippines Islands." Adams to Storey, Aug. 22, 1902, box 3, Welsh Papers, Michigan. For more on the committee, see Adams to Norton, May 2, 1902, Adams Papers, MHS. In the spring of 1902, the composition of the committee appears to have been different—with Moorfield Storey in the place of Andrew Carnegie, and including a Finance Committee of George Foster Peabody and William H. Baldwin, Jr. Herbert Welsh wrote that "The work of our Committee is to gather witnesses, to sift evidence, and to present such material to the Investigating Committee of the Senate, to throw light on all that is hidden in this business, and to secure in the Philippines themselves, by the demand of an irresistible popular sentiment, a rigid investigation of conditions which exist there." Welsh to Lewis, May 16, 1902, box 1, Welsh Papers, Michigan.

145. On the unreliability of sources, see Adams to Welsh, May 9, 1902, box 1, Welsh Papers, Michigan; Adams to Culberson, May 7, 1902, Adams Papers, MHS; Adams to Schurz, July 1, 1902, Adams Papers, MHS; Welsh to Adams, May 8, 1902, Adams Papers, MHS. Perhaps Norton expressed the sentiment best when, writing to Herbert Welsh, he noted that "I do not think we should be content with a military investigation conducted under the authority of Secretary Root. His duplicity in the matter of the Philippine atrocities, and his recent eulogistic adulation of Senator Platt suffice to destroy all confidence in him." Norton to Welsh, Apr. 17, 1902, box 1, Welsh Papers, Michigan. On sending an agent and on H. Parker Willis as the ideal person to conduct the investigation, see Storey to Palmer, July 28, 1903, box 1, Welsh Papers, Michigan; Adams to Schurz, Aug. 7, 1902, Adams Papers, MHS; Adams to Schurz, Aug. 13, 1902, Adams Papers, MHS; Adams to Davison, Oct. 27, 1904, Adams Papers, MHS. Willis himself made a case for funding an investigation at least once, Willis to Welsh, [undated, probably 1901?], box 2, Welsh Papers, Michigan.

146. Adams to Schurz, May 8, 1902, Adams Papers, MHS; Storey to Sniffen, June 3, 1904, box 2, Welsh Papers, Michigan.

147. Willis to Storey, May 12, 1904, Storey Papers, LOC. These reports were sent per instruction: "The objects and methods of our mission have been already sufficiently discussed. If you go, you will go simply as a traveller seeking information, and have it distinctly understood you are not in correspondence with any newspaper. You are merely passing the winter in the Philippines for your information, and not improbably with a view of publishing the result of your observations. These, however, would be transmitted to us frequently. In other words, you would collect your material as you went along, and forward it in the form of letters to those who sent you out." Campbell to Willis, Oct. 14,

1903, box 1, Welsh Papers, Michigan.

148. Willis to Storey et al, Sept. 22, 1904, Storey Papers, LOC.

149. Willis to Storey, June 23, 1904, Storey Papers, LOC; Willis to Storey, July 8, 1904, Storey Papers, LOC; Willis to Storey, Sept. 12, 1904, Storey Papers, LOC.

150. Willis to Storey, July 19, 1904, Storey Papers, LOC; Willis to Storey, June 4, 1904, Storey Papers, LOC; Willis to Storey, May 27, 1904, Storey Papers, LOC. In his May 27, 1904 letter to Moorfield Storey, Willis summarized: "On the whole, I feel that our general policy and its effects on the islands have been worse by far than I had supposed. On the other hand, I believe that, so far as not inconsistent with their political well-being, some of the men at the head are doing what they can to furnish a good administration. The problems are too tough for them, however, and I feel that the whole government, with here and there an exception, may properly be styled incompetent. The Taft cult shrinks to wonderfully small proportions when viewed from close at hand and I believe his alleged popularity was purely fictitious."

151. See Willis's report on finding a publisher: Willis to Storey, Mar. 26, 1905, Storey Papers, LOC. On personal attacks, see Willis to Adams, Nov. 2, 1904, Adams Papers, MHS; Adams to Willis, Nov. 4, 1904, Adams Papers, MHS; Willis to Adams, Dec. 3, 1904, Adams Papers, MHS.

152. H. Parker Willis, *Our Philippine Problem: A Study of American Colonial Policy* (New York: Henry Holt and Company, 1905), 454.

153. Adams to Lodge, Oct. 3, 1902, Adams Papers, MHS; Adams to Schurz, Oct. 25, 1904, Adams Papers, MHS.

154. LeRoy travelogue, Oct. 17, 1901, LeRoy Papers, BHL. LeRoy continued: "Ex-Lieu. W.F. Pack, of Michigan, who came from Hong Kong on the same boat, told Professor Worcester that Warren had a load of Lopez's speeches and other like documents in his baggage, and that he said he was coming here "to see why he was paying a war tax."

155. Taft to Root, Oct. 14, 1901, reel 464, Taft Papers, LOC.

156. McIntyre to Ide, June 23, 1906, outgoing letters, RG 350, NACP. In 1911, the BIA still kept tabs on the activities of the Anti-Imperialist League. Dinwiddie wrote to Worcester that, though a project to educate Americans about the Philippines was nixed by the BIA leadership, it was not ended before he had the opportunity to collect "over 60,000 words of publicity" that shed a favorable light on Worcester and "holds up to ridicule the Anti-Imperialist League's propaganda," Dinwiddie to Worcester, May 23, 1911, box 1, Dean C. Worcester Papers, BHL. Worcester's contempt for any anti-

imperialist impulse is well-documented, such as when he notes that "our anti-imperialist friends will insist upon making idiots of themselves." Worcester to Beal, Apr. 24, 1911, box 3, Junius E. Beal Papers, BHL.

157. Javier Borres y Romero, *The Philippine Insurrection: The Four* Truths, trans. Rosa Maria M. Icagasi (Manila: Toyota Foundation/UP Press, 2002).

158. Scott Nearing, *The American Empire* (New York: Rand School of Social Science, 1921), 23.

159. Taft to Root, Dec. 14, 1900, reel 463, Taft Papers, LOC. In a letter to Edward Colston, Taft elaborated on this point, observing that "The experience of nine months now under a military government convinces me that an army officer, whether he be the subject of the Czar of Russia or a citizen of the United States is not adapted to conduct the affairs of a civil government." Taft to Colston, Apr. 24, 1901, reel 32, Taft Papers, LOC. See also Taft to Root, July 26, 1900, reel 463, Taft Papers, LOC; and Taft to Wilcox, Sept. 24, 1901, reel 33, Taft Papers, LOC. On the provincial level, governor of Tayabas wrote to Taft, "I have endeavored to state truthfully the difficulties that civil government encounters by reason of the attitude of the officers of the Army. In doing so I feel that should my report be made public I will have the whole army against me. But I believe it is my duty to tell the truth and take the consequences whatever they may be." Gardener to Taft, Dec. 16, 1901, reel 34, Taft Papers, LOC.

160. Forestry Bureau, Philippine Islands, *Spanish Public Land Laws in the Philippine Islands and their History to August 13,* 1898 (Washington: Government Printing Office, 1901), 54.

161. Jose S. Reyes, *Legislative History of American Economic Policy toward the Philippines* (New York: Columbia University, 1923), 172.

162. Charles Parkhurst warned, "I have been reading recently the book entitled 'A Century of Dishonor' which details with blood-curdling particularity the steps by which for a hundred years we have been trying to 'elevate' the aborigines of this country. And there is no reason to suppose that we shall be any less heathenism in our dealings with savages around the other side of the globe than we are with those at home, in fact the more remote our government officials the less there can be expected of them, for it is by so much the harder to watch them, and watching an American official is the only way to keep him from devouring the people he is paid to take care of. There is no leech that will draw more blood or leave less life. So long as it is an understood thing that the office is spoils we may well pray to be delivered from the responsibility of governing dependencies." Parkhurst, 15-16. Natives fighting in the Philippines also noted this parallel; Lukban wrote, "Liberty

and independence being then the very pure ideal which we are all pursuing, join me in the field so as to expel these deceitful Yankees, for they have come with the intention of exterminating us later, as they exterminated the Indians of America, who were the real owners of that land, and rather than have this happen to us, before a large number of Americans arrives, let us hurl ourselves against these who are already here, and let us wage a war without quarter against these heartless vandals; for when a people united as brothers are defending themselves, there is no army strong enough to conquer them. It is only necessary to note the striking example of our brothers of Luzon, who preferred to have their towns reduced to ashes and their residents corpses rather than surrender. To-day Luzon is already independent, already enjoys the sweets of liberty, the fruit of four years' constant warfare. Let us imitate them and let us persevere in the struggle until the longed-for independence is attained. "Lukban to the local presidentes of this province of Samar, Mountains of Samar, Exhibit 1323, Feb. 4, 1900," in *Philippine Insurrection against the United States,* ed. Taylor, 5:637-8.

163. See, for example, Storey and Winslow to Taft, Dec. 20, 1911, vol. 4, Winslow papers, Michigan.

164. D.R. Williams, "Operation of 'Land Registration Act," *Official* Gazette, Apr. 15, 1903, 257.

165. Reynaldo Ileto, *Knowing America's Colony: A Hundred Years from the Philippine War,* Honolulu: Center for Philippine Studies, 1999.

166. The problems of the Bureau of Public Lands were not limited to a population averse to its programs, but also to internal factors. In addition to anecdotal evidence of the inadequacy of workers in the colonial government service, there is indication of this in the passage of Philippine Commission Act 876 on September 9, 1903, which including a section on "levying a penalty upon notary publics who fail to enter in the certification of instruments acknowledged by them the number, place of issue, and date of the cedula certificate of each of the parties to said instruments."

167. "Rules and Regulations of the Court of Land Registration of the Philippine Islands," *Official Gazette,* July 8, 1903, 481-2.

168. D.R. Williams, "Operation of 'Land Registration Act'," *Official Gazette,* Apr. 15, 1903, 257.

169. Ibid.

170. Philippine Commission Act 1128 (Apr. 28, 1904), An Act prescribing regulations governing the procedure for acquiring title to public coal lands in the Philippine Islands.

171. Bureau of Public Lands, "Circular of Information, January 20, 1905," *Official Gazette*, Mar. 1, 1905, 99.

172. To facilitate the bureau's execution of its expanded duties, the Philippine Commission passed Act 1491 on May 22, 1906, "providing for the education of Filipino students as surveyors."

173. On drawing from the work of others, see Sanger to U.S. Secretary of the Interior Hitchcock, Jan. 9, 1902, outgoing letters, RG 350, NACP; Sanger to U.S. Secretary of the Interior Hitchcock, Jan. 24, 1902, outgoing letters, RG 350, NACP; Sanger to U.S. Secretary of the Interior Hitchcock, Sept. 4, 1902, outgoing letters, RG 350, NACP; Sanger to U.S. Secretary of the Interior Hitchcock, Sept. 30, 1902, outgoing letters, RG 350, NACP; Taft to Frear, Sept. 14, 1900, reel 31, Taft Papers, LOC; Carpenter to Tipton, Oct. 3, 1901, reel 33, Taft Papers, LOC; Tipton to Carpenter, Oct. 12, 1901, reel 33, Taft Papers, LOC.

174. Executive Order 31 (June 29, 1906).

175. On August 3, 1908, Governor-General Smith signed Executive Order 80 requiring the assistance of bureaus in the Bureau of Coast and Geodetic Survey's efforts to make maps of the archipelago, by transmitting "a copy of all geographical information, including descriptive reports, which may have been collected by them or under their direction, including a copy of all maps or sketches which may have been prepared." Philippine Commission Act 2325, passed on February 19, 1914, specified the public notices required for sale of lands; these specifications suggest not only the volume of records the new land laws mandated, but also the scope of regulations that the Bureau of Public Lands was required by law to ensure, namely published notice once a week for 6 consecutive weeks, in 2 newspapers, one in Manila and one (if there is one) near the land, one in English in an English-language paper, and one in Spanish in a Spanish-language paper, and at least 10 days after the last published notice, a notice posted near the land.

176. Apr. 22, 1911, Forbes Journals, MHS. Forbes' eagerness to "vivify the whole agricultural life of the islands" by land registration and titles is expressed in his journal entry of September 17, 1910.

177. Philippine Legislature Act No. 2222 (Feb. 3, 1913), "An act further to amend section thirty-three, chapter four of act numbered nine hundred and twenty-six, entitled 'The Public Land Act,' as amended, by providing for the granting of free patents to native settlers until January first, nineteen hundred and twenty-three."

178. Winslow to Welsh, Mar. 15, 1900, Welsh Papers, Michigan.

179. Edwards to Smith, May 16, 1908, outgoing letters, RG 350, NACP.

180. Edwards to Forbes, Apr. 19, 1910, outgoing letters, RG 350, NACP.

181. McIntyre to Gilbert, May 23, 1912, outgoing letters, RG 350, NACP. Manuel Quezon agreed; see Quezon to Jones, Feb. 14, 1912, reel 2, Quezon Papers, BHL.

182. McIntyre to Barrows, July 21, 1910, outgoing letters, RG 350, NACP.

183. Anti-Imperialist League to Taft, Dec. 30, 1911, Winslow Papers, Michigan. The decision to send this letter is noted in the Executive Committee meeting minutes of the Anti-Imperialist League, Dec. 28, 1911, Winslow Papers, Michigan.

184. Quezon and Osmena to Garrison, Apr. 29, 1913, reel 3, Quezon Papers, BHL; Quezon to Winslow, May 18, 1912, reel 2, Quezon Papers, BHL.

185. Quezon to Jones, Feb. 14, 1912, reel 2, Quezon papers, BHL. Complaints from tenants are also referenced in McIntyre to Governor-General, Feb. 3, 1911, outgoing letters, RG 350, NACP. In his "Disposition of the Friar Lands" in the House of Representatives, Quezon sounded what would become his familiar call for Philippine independence: "If to be free we must keep the Philippines undeveloped, if to be free we must refuse to admit foreign capital into the islands, if to be free we must be poor and remain poor, we will unanimously and unhesitatingly prefer to be poor but free, than to be rich but subjects." Manuel Quezon, *Disposition of the Friar Lands* (Washington: Government Printing Office, 1912), 16.

186. Quezon to Martin, Jan. 10, 1914, reel 4, Quezon Papers, BHL.

187. Worcester to Reighard, Dec. 12, 1910, box 6, Jacob Ellsworth Reighard Papers, BHL.

188. David P. Barrows, "The Governor-General of the Philippines under Spain and the United States," *The Pacific Ocean in History*, ed. H. Morse Stephens and Herbert E. Bolton (New York: The MacMillan Company, 1917), 254-5.

189. Barrows to Taft, Feb. 11, 1902, reel 4, Taft papers, LOC.

190. Department of Interior, Bureau of Public Lands, Philippine Islands, *Primer Containing Questions and Answers on the Public Land Laws in Force in the Philippine Islands* (Manila: Government Printing Office, 1906), 4.

191. Ibid., 13.

192. The report noted: "Under the Spanish system orders of sale could be made upon petition of private parties or at the instance of the administration. Only residents of the Philippine Islands could acquire land, and all land was saleable, except those that had

passed to private ownership, those belonging to forest zones and those which were found within a limit of the commons belonging to towns or within zones which had been granted to the towns for the use of the people.

193. To obtain a free patent, a Filipino must have lived on and cultivated the land "From August 1, 1898, to the present time. If his ancestors have occupied and cultivated the land during part of this time and he the rest of the time, he is entitled to a free patent. Also, if he and his ancestors continuously occupied and cultivated the land from August 1, 1895, to August 1, 1898, and from July 4, 1902 to July 26, 1904, he may claim a free patent, even if he and his ancestors did not live on the land between August 1, 1898, and July 4, 1902." Philippines, Department of Interior, Bureau of Public Lands, *Primer*, 5.

194. Ibid., 6.

195. Ibid., 7.

196. See, for example, Hamilton Wright et al, *America Across the Seas: Our Colonial Empire* (New York: C.S. Hammond and Company, 1909), 13. Wright observed, "Those men of our early West who divided their time between shooting the skulking Indians and cultivating their crops were not greater pioneers than the soldier boys in the Philippines who have turned farmers. But the white man has not proved a ménage to his Malay brothers. The population of the Philippines has increased twelvefold since the Spaniards came. While, on the other hand, the American Indians either perished in resisting civilization or in succumbing to it, the Malay profits by contact with civilization."

197. Kiefer to Secretary of State, Apr. 15, 1899; Beebe to Secretary of State, July 13, 1899; Wheatley to Secretary of State, Sept. 20, 1899; Sprague to War Department, Nov. 17, 1899; Goodell to President, Dec. 3, 1899; Peer to Treasury Department, Jan. 4, 1900; Schwartz to War Department, Dec. 19, 1899; Wright to War Department, Jan. 30, 1899; Denkhaus to War Department, Sept. 10, 1900. File 212, RG 350, NACP. After the conclusion of the Spanish-American war, the BIA received "a great many inquiries" about land concessions to honorably discharged veterans of that war, McIntyre to Smith, Oct. 8, 1909, outgoing letters, RG 350, NACP. In 1908, the *Far Eastern Review* reported the prospect of "the installation of a modern amusement park in Manila," using capital from businessmen in both the Philippines and the United States. "Manila's Coney Island," *Far Eastern Review* 5, no. 5 (Oct. 1908), 170-71.

198. A Bureau of Lands primer on public lands offered only this: "The public lands have not been surveyed under either Spanish or American rule. Therefore, it is not known exactly where they are. You may find out by asking the old residents of a town. You may also learn something from the old "Registro de Propiedad" and the "Register of Deeds"

now kept. Here you may find whether the land has been registered. The provincial treasurer will tell you if the land has ever been taxed. If not, it is probably public land. Philippines, Department of Interior, Bureau of Public Lands, Primer, 11. This was reiterated in "Our Public Land," *Far Eastern Review* 2, no. 3 (Aug. 1905), 58-59.

199. Bureau of Archives, Philippine Islands, *Special Report of the Chief of the Bureau of Archives to the Honorable Civil Governor through the Secretary of Public Instruction: Lands of Arroceros and Aguados* (Manila: Bureau of Public Printing, 1904).

200. Philippines, Department of Interior, Bureau of Public Lands, *Primer*, 10.

201. Ibid., 15.

202. Ibid., 17.

203. Ibid. See also Travelogue, Apr. 25, 1901, LeRoy Papers, BHL.

204. The friction between Chief of the Bureau of Agriculture Frank Lamson-Scribner and the Secretary of the Interior, Dean Worcester, to whom he reported is well documented, at least from Lamson-Scribner's point of view, and resulted in the Philippine Commission's request for his resignation, Taft to Lamson-Scribner, Feb. 24, 1904, box 4, Lamson-Scribner Papers, LOC. Writing of Worcester, Lamson-Scribner observed that, "He is a man for whom I have no respect in any capacity, and is a dangerous man to be given so much power as the Commissioners possess." Lamson-Scribner to Galloway, Oct. 15, 1903, box 3, Lamson-Scribner Papers, LOC. For more descriptions of his working conditions in the Philippines, see Lamson-Scribner to Galloway, May 30, 1903, box 3; Lamson-Scribner to Wilson, June 10, 1903, box 3; and Lamson-Scribner to Galloway, Apr. 19, 1903, box 3, Lamson-Scribner Papers, LOC.

205. The scrapbook collection of Archibald Ward, an American veterinarian sent to the Philippines to see to the epidemic, neatly captures the scope and tenor of media coverage in the Philippines. In addition to reportage of measures considered and taken, local outlets analyzed, critiqued, and sometimes praised administration for its efforts; discussion of possible remedies, the extent of the problem, and its causes were also routine. See Archibald R. Ward Papers, #6596, RMC.

206. Report of the Acting Chief of the Bureau of Archives, Patents, Copyrights, and Trade-Marks, Sept. 13, 1904, RG 350, NACP.

207. Report of the Bureau of Archives, Patents, Copyrights, and Trade-Marks, Aug. 15, 1905, RG 350, NACP. Yriarte further reported that "Four hundred thirteen municipalities have not yet sent in their brands and the brands of the private citizens resident within their jurisdictional limits." The registration of cattle gradually picked up momentum, and for

the year 1905-1906, 10,998 brands had been registered. In the year 1907-1908, 13,000 brands were registered, while 31,796 were received and 124 returned for correction. In the year 1908-1909, 28,000 brands were registered, while 18,620 were received and 1,255 returned for correction. In the year 1909-1910, 30,000 brands were registered, while 17,569 were received and 353 returned for correction. In 1911-1912, 14,647 brands were received, and of these, 2,460 were returned for correction. In 1915-1916, 18,000 brands were registered, while 19,875 brands were received and 1,950 returned for correction. These numbers not only show the number of brands registered and the number of records in need of correction; they also illustrate the bureau's back-log of work in this aspect.

208. Report of the Executive Secretary, Sept. 1, 1906, RG 350, NACP. Fergusson named only Rizal and Bulacan as being sites of operation for the scheme but suggested that it also occurred in other provinces surrounding Manila. Fergusson renewed his call for legislation to address cattle stealing in his 1907 report, *Report of the Executive Secretary*, Oct. 20, 1907, RG 350, NACP.

209. Report of the Chief of Archives, Patents, Copyrights, and Trade-Marks, 1909, RG 350, NACP.

210. Report of the Chief of the Division of Archives, Patents, Copyrights, and Trade-marks, 1910, RG 350, NACP. Despite these measures, the annual report of this year states that the situation had not been entirely remedied. In fact, Yriarte notes that recent developments showed that "notwithstanding the said ordinance, which restricts the registration in this capital [Manila] of cattle coming from the provinces, in order to prevent thefts, these continue to the detriment of the agriculture. It is hoped, however, that this state of affairs will disappear very soon, in view of the activity with which the provincial and municipal authorities and other agents of the Government endeavor to remedy the same by eliminating the persons who make their living in this reprobate manner."

211. This configuration of the committee was not permanent. With Executive Order 27 (Sept. 25, 1905), Sixto S. Sandejas replaced Burgos. With the issuance of Executive Order 53 (June 23, 1917), the committee consisted of the Secretary of the Interior (chair), Director of Coast Surveys, Chief of the Executive Bureau, Director of Education, Director of Public Lands, Director of the Bureau of Science, and Director of Posts.

212. This expansion of the responsibilities of the Board of Geographical Names seems to have conflicted with those of the Philippine Committee on Geographical Names, as the latter continued to publish its decisions on geographical names even after Executive Order 399 went into effect.

213. Executive Order 493 (Aug. 10, 1906), called for the renaming and expanded responsibility of the United States Geographic Board. Executive Order 3206 (Dec. 30, 1919) called for the creation of the Board of Surveys and Maps.

214. William Tipton, Secretary of the Philippine Committee on Geographical Names, to Editor of the *Official Gazette*, Feb. 6, 1905, *Official Gazette*, Mar. 1, 1905.

215. Decisions of Feb. 6, 1905, published in *Official Gazette,* Mar. 1, 1905; decisions of July 12, 1905, published in *Official Gazette,* Aug. 9, 1905; decisions of Sept. 6, 1905, published in *Official Gazette*, Sept. 25, 1906; decisions of Feb.7, 1906, published in *Official* Gazette, Mar. 21, 1906; decisions of Jan. 3,1906, published in *Official Gazette,* Jan. 17, 1906; decisions of Sept. 14, 1910, published in *Official Gazette*, Oct. 19 and Nov. 9, 1910; decisions of Oct. 3 and 4, 1917, published in *Official Gazette*, Nov. 7, 1917; decisions of Nov. 7, 1917, published in *Official Gazette*, Nov. 28, 1917; decisions of Dec. 5, 1917, published in *Official Gazette*, Dec. 19, 1917; decisions of Mar. 6, 1918, published in *Official Gazette*, Apr. 3, 1918; decisions of July 10, 1918, published in *Official Gazette*, Sept. 11, 1918; decisions of Sept. 4, 1918, published in *Official Gazette*, Sept. 25, 1918; decisions of Oct. 2, 1918, published in *Official Gazette*, Oct. 23, 1918; decisions of Nov. 6, 1918, published in *Official Gazette*, Jan. 1, 1919; decisions of Jan. 8, 1919, published in *Official Gazette*, Jan. 29, 1919; decisions of Feb. 5, 1919, published in *Official Gazette*, Feb. 26, 1919.

216. Executive Order 52 (Dec. 10, 1906) introduced a particular "form and style of printed envelope shall be used by all Bureaus and Offices of the Insular Government"; Executive Order 77 (July 28, 1908) directed that the metric system should be used in all official documents; Executive Order 47 (Aug. 22, 1912) depicted the signs used by the United States Geographical Board, to be adopted by the Government of the Philippine Islands; Executive Order 8 (Jan. 16, 1917) described the courses through the colonial government for official mail; the text of Executive Order 39 (Oct. 19, 1906) reads: "It having been observed that in official documents the Philippine Commission is variously referred to as 'Comision Legislativa de Filipinas,' 'Comision Civil,' or 'Comision en Filipinas,' notice is hereby given that the official name of said body is, in English, 'Philippine Commission' and, in Spanish, 'Comision de Filipinas.'"

217. Maximo M. Kalaw, *The Case for the Filipinos* (New York: Century, 1916), xiii.

218. For a concise chronological account of these changes in Philippine colonial government, see: Teodoro A. Agoncillo, *History of the Filipino People* (Quezon City: Garotech Publishing [1960], 2006), 307-13.

219. Worcester, *Conditions in the Philippines*, 17.

220. Manuel Quezon was also critical of Worcester. In a speech delivered on October 12, 1914, Quezon was precise in disapproval: "Both the policy of economy and that of doing justice to the Filipino people provoked a storm of criticism on the part of the necessary victims of such a policy, and Governor General Harrison was accused of disorganizing the Philippine Government, of disregarding the civil-service rules, and of using the methods of the ward politician. An article purporting to be an interview with Governor General Harrison saw the light in a Honolulu newspaper. This was quoted and requited and several times reprinted to show that Governor General Harrison was an ordinary politician, to be ranked with those who believe in and practice the spoils system in the most extreme form. One of the most notorious occasions on which use was made of this supposed interview was the citation of it by ex-Secretary Dean C. Worcester, formerly of the Philippine government, in his book entitled "The Philippines—Past and Present," published after the Philippine Islands had been relieved of his authority." Manuel Quezon, *The Jones Philippine Bill* (Washington: Government Printing Office, 1914), 76.

221. Moses to Taft, Jan. 22, 1903, Taft Papers, LOC. Moses' request for a copy of the minutes was approved by the Philippine Commission on February 3, 1904, in the Executive Minutes of the United States Philippine Commission, Sept. 1, 1903 – Sept. 1, 1904, page 480. After receiving the minutes, Moses reflected, "As I review some of Paterno's operations, I am almost persuaded that I ought to attempt to make a comic opera rather than a sober historical statement." Moses to Taft, Mar. 7, 1904, Taft Papers, LOC.

222. David P. Barrows, *A History of the Philippines* (New York: American Book Company, 1905), 3.

223. David P. Barrows, *A Decade of American Government in the Philippines, 1903-1913* (New York: World Book Company, 1914), xiv. Daniel Williams, who served as private secretary to Bernard Moses and later as Associate Judge in the Philippine Court of Land Registration, also wrote about the early years of colonial civil rule: Daniel Williams, *The Odyssey of the Philippine Commission* (Chicago: McClurg, 1913).

224. Kalaw, *Case for the* Filipinos, xi-xii. William Jones provided a complementary analysis a few years earlier, noting that to critics of United States rule in the islands, "the reply has always been glibly made, as if that were sufficient in itself to disarm criticism and forever silence all complaint, that within the past ten years public schools have greatly multiplied in the Philippines; that the inhabitants of the islands have made wonderful progress in the acquisition of knowledge of various kinds that sanitary conditions have improved; and that many important public works have been inaugurated as a result of our beneficent rule. The Filipino who does not accept this reply as conclusive of the question is frequently denounced as an ingrate. Indeed, his failure to accept such reasoning as

conclusive is cited as evidence of his incapacity for self-government." Jones, 9.

225. To express his support of the colonial government's reorganization, Governor-General Francis Burton Harrison signed Executive Order 22 on March 28, 1916.

226. Severino Velasco, "The National Library," in *Focus on the National Library: A Compilation of Papers Presented during an Orientation Seminar on the Policies and Functions of the National Library, September 7-10, 1964*, ed. Abraham de Guzman (Manila: The National Library, 1964), 4.

227. For an overview of these predecessor organizations, see: Cheryl Beredo, "Import of the Archive: American Colonial Bureaucracy in the Philippines, 1898-1916," Ph.D. dissertation, University of Hawai'i, 74-90.

228. McKee to Robertson, Apr. 16, 1919, box 12, Robertson Papers, LOC.

229. The full quote from McKee's letter to Robertson reads: "Our dear Bessie Agnes is leaving the Islands for good! She is not going because she wants to either but because she has come to the end of her tether, and the government thinks it can worry along without her. It is the outcome of Mrs. Elmer's insistence, and though she too was obliged to sever her connection with the library she thinks it was well worth it. B.A.D. is leaving very soon—within a week I think. She seems to have nothing special in view for the future, but it has been suggested that she will lead the life literary in the future and the library staff gave her a handsome desk set on the strength of it when the despadidoed (is that permissable [sic]?) of her. If she had gone to the stage now there might have been some hope, or the lecture platform would have been a good field, but I can't think there is much of a future in the library line for Bess. Speaking of literature—there is a choice piece enclosed which gives a history of the Library, but it fails to mention either you or Mrs. Elmer or me or any of our work, which goes to show what nonentities we were. I have had neither the time nor the courage to go into the library since I came back. I feel it is just a monument to wasted endeavor." McKee to Robertson, Apr. 16, 1919, box 12, Robertson Papers, LOC.

230. McKee to Robertson, Feb. 27, 1916, box 6, Robertson Papers, LOC; McKee to Robertson, Feb. 28, 1916, box 6, Robertson Papers, LOC; McKee to Robertson, May 1, 1916, box 6, Robertson Papers, LOC.

231. Kalaw to Winslow, Oct. 10, 1913, reel 4, Quezon Papers, BHL. Further, Kalaw opined. "He was practically, outside of the President, the one person responsible for the appointment of the Governor."

232. Catechism of Marquardt, page 216, box 5, Walter Marquardt Papers, BHL.

233. Bell to Wood, Dec. 5, 1913, box 218, Leonard Wood Papers, LOC.

234. Bandholtz to Harvey, Jan. 18, 1913, reel 5, Harry Bandholtz Papers, BHL.

235. Worcester to *The New York Times*, Mar. 16, 1914, vol. 6, Worcester Papers, Michigan.

236. Taft to Worcester, Feb. 17, 1915, vol. 5, Worcester Papers, Michigan; Heiser to Worcester, Jan. 18, 1915, Robertson to Worcester, May 31, 1914, vol. 6, Worcester Papers, Michigan.

237. Forbes to Garrison, Aug. 25, 1913, box 592, entry 5, RG 350, NACP.

238. On September 4, 1913, Forbes wrote: "Well, my nine years of smoke and roar are over and I am a private citizen again. My secret ambition all these years has been to get back just where I am now—free-footed, my work behind, and an opportunity to do things from behind the scenes. I've told everyone they needed expect ever to hear of me again, as I want to retire. [...] President Wilson's letter didn't help the situation in Manila at all. People got madder and madder over the clumsy and gauche way my removal was brought about, and cables to this effect were sent to the States. I was sorry afterward that I'd let McIntyre's foolish cable be published; I think it would have been bigger to have withheld it." Forbes goes on to describe how he won again, by publicly stating that he was not offended by the new administration's desire to oust him and thus winning over public opinion. Forbes Journals, MHS.

239. Putnam quoted in Root to Taft, reel 38, Taft Papers, LOC.

240. "Appendix C, Report of the Chief of the Bureau of Archives, Patents, Copyrights and Trademarks, 1905" RG 350, NACP; "Report of the Executive Secretary to the Governor-General, 1907," RG 350, NACP.

241. Theodore Roosevelt Schellenberg, *Modern Archives: Principles and Techniques* (Chicago: University of Chicago Press, 1956).

BIBLIOGRAPHY

Primary Sources

Manuscripts and Archives

American Historical Collection, Ateneo de Manila University (AHC)
United States Military Governor in the Philippine Islands. General Orders, 1899-1900.
United States Philippine Commission. Executive Minutes, September 1, 1901-February 1, 1902.
United States Philippine Commission. Public Minutes, 1900-1907.

Bentley Historical Library, University of Michigan (BHL)
Bandholtz, Harry. Papers.
Beal, Junius E. Papers.
LeRoy, James Alfred. Papers.
Marquardt, Walter. Papers.
Quezon, Manuel Luis. Papers.
Reighard, Jacob Ellsworth. Papers.
Worcester, Dean C. Papers.

Division of Rare and Manuscript Collections, Cornell University Library (RMC)
Schurman, Jacob Gould. Papers.
Ward, Archibald R. Papers.

Division of Manuscripts, Library of Congress (LOC)
Lamson-Scribner, F. Papers.
Robertson, James A. Papers
Storey, Moorfield. Papers.
Taft, William Howard. Papers.
Taylor, John R.M. Papers.
Wood, Leonard. Papers

Massachusetts Historical Society (MHS)
Adams, Charles Francis, II. Papers.
Atkinson, Edward. Papers
Edwards, Clarence Ransom. Papers

Forbes, W. Cameron. Papers.
Hoar, George Frisbie. Papers.
Lodge, Henry Cabot. Papers.
Whiting, Jasper. Papers.
Winslow, Erving. Papers.

Special Collections Library, University of Michigan (Michigan)
Welsh, Herbert. Papers.
Winslow, Erving. Papers.
Worcester, Dean. Papers.

National Archives Building, Washington, DC (NAB)
United States Army Overseas Operations and Commands. Records, 1898-1942.

National Archives at College Park, MD (NACP)
Bureau of Insular Affairs. Records.

Published Sources

Insular Government Documents
Bureau of Archives. Philippine Islands. *Special Report of the Chief of the Bureau of Archives to the Honorable Civil Governor through the Secretary of Public Instruction: Lands of Arroceros and Aguados.* Manila: Bureau of Public Printing, 1904.
Bureau of Education. Philippine Islands. *The Industrial Museum, Library, and Exhibits of the Bureau of Education.* Manila: Bureau of Printing, 1913.
–––. *Libraries for Philippine Public Schools.* Manila: Bureau of Printing, 1912.
–––. *A Statement of Organization, Aims and Conditions of Service in the Bureau of Education.* Manila: Bureau of Printing, 1911.
Department of Interior. Bureau of Public Lands. Philippine Islands. *Primer Containing Questions and Answers on the Public Land Laws in Force in the Philippine Islands.* Manila: Government Printing Office, 1906.
Everett, Colson. *A Special Report of the Investigation of the Philippine General Hospital,* Manila: Bureau of Printing, 1916.
Forestry Bureau. Philippine Islands. *Spanish Public Land Laws in the Philippine Islands and their History to August 13, 1898.* Washington: Government Printing Office, 1901.
Philippine Islands. *Official Gazette,* 1902-1919.

Periodicals and Books

Allen, Andrew Hussey. "The Historical Archives of the Department of State." *Annual Report of the American Historical Association* (1895): 281-98.

American Historical Association. *Annual Report of the American Historical* Association, 1895-1911.

———. "Proceedings of the First Annual Conference of Archivists." *Annual Report of the American Historical Association* (1909): 337-78.

American Imperialism and the Philippine Insurrection: Testimony Taken from Hearings on Affairs in the Philippine Islands before the Senate Committee on the Philippines, 1902. Boston: Little, Brown, and Co., 1969.

Andrews, Charles. "Archives." *Annual Report of the American Historical Association* (1913): 262-65.

Anti-Imperialist League. *Philippine Independence: Discussion of Hon. W.H. Taft's Letter, March 16, 1905.* Boston: Anti-Imperialist League, 1905.

Apacible, Galicano. *To the American People.* Toronto, 1900.

Archives of Government Offices Outside of the City of Washington. Washington: Government Printing Office, 1913.

Barrows, David P. *A Decade of American Government in the Philippines, 1903-1913.* New York: World Book Company, 1914.

———. "The Governor-General of the Philippines under Spain and the United States." In *The Pacific Ocean in History*, edited by H. Morse Stephens and Herbert E. Bolton, 238-268. New York: The MacMillan Company, 1917.

———. *A History of the Philippines.* New York: American Book Company, 1905.

Bartlett, Richard. *Remarks and Documents Related to the Preservation and Keeping of the Public Archives.* Concord: Asa McFarland, 1837.

Bear, Estella Adelaide. *Where are Our Nation's Credentials?* Camden, NJ, 1916.

Betts, W. Colgrove. "The Philadelphia Commercial Museum." *The Journal of Political Economy* 8, no. 2 (March 1900). http://www.jstor.org/stable/1817336

Borres y Romero, Javier. *The Philippine Insurrection: The Four Truths.* Translated by Rosa Maria M. Icagasi. Manila: Toyota Foundation/UP Press, 2002.

Bourne, Henry E. "The Work of the American Historical Societies." *Annual Report of the American Historical Association* (1904): 117-27.

Carnegie, Andrew. "Should the United States Expand?" In *Republic or Empire? The Philippine Question*, 89-99. Chicago: The Independence Company, 1899.

Curtis, George William. "This Year's Work in Civil Reform." *Proceedings of the Annual Meeting of the National Civil Service Reform League* (1882): 3-20.

Daniel, John. "The Effect of Annexation of the Philippines on American Labor." In *Republic or Empire? The Philippine Question*, 367-425. Chicago: The

Independence Company, 1899.

Dickinson, Jacob M. *Address delivered by the Honorable Jacob M. Dickinson at the Banquet of the Industrial Club of Chicago, Congress Hotel, Chicago, Saturday Evening, February 28, 1914.* [Chicago, 1914?].

Edwards, Clarence. "Governing the Philippine Islands." *National Geographic* 15 (July 1904): 284.

"Failure of the Manila Strike," *Far Eastern Review* 5, no. 11 (Apr. 1909): 375.

Ford, Worthington Chauncey. "Public Records in Our Dependencies." *Annual Report of the American Historical Association* (1904): 131-47.

Freitag, Joseph Kendall. *The Fireproofing of Steel Buildings.* New York: John Wiley and Sons, 1906.

Gantenbein, C.U., comp. *The Official Records of the Oregon Volunteers in the Spanish War and Philippine Insurrection.* Salem, OR: J.R. Whitney, 1903.

Gompers, Samuel. "Imperialism: Dangers and Wrongs." In *Republic or Empire? The Philippine Question*, 209-11. Chicago: The Independence Company, 1899.

Hoar, George Frisbie. *Speech of Honorable George Frisbie Hoar, of Massachusetts, in the Senate of the United States, May 22, 1902.* Washington: Government Printing Office, 1902.

"Industrial Education in the Philippines." *Science* 36, no. 926 (Sept. 27, 1912): 396-7.

Jones, William A. *Misgovernment in the Philippines and Cost to the United States of American Occupation: Speech of Hon. William A. Jones of Virginia in the House of Representatives, January 28, 1913.* Washington: Government Printing Office, 1913.

Jordan, David Starr. *The Question of the Philippines.* Palo Alto, CA: Graduate Club, 1899.

Kalaw, Maximo M. *The Case for the Filipinos.* New York: Century, 1916.

Leland, Waldo G. "The Archives of the Federal Government." *Records of the Columbia Historical Society* 11 (1908): 71-100.

---. "The National Archives: A Programme" *American Historical Review* 18 (1912): 1-28.

---. "Some Fundamental Principles in Relation to Archives." *Annual Report of the American Historical Association* (1912): 264-8.

"Manila's Coney Island." *Far Eastern Review* 5, no. 3 (Oct. 1908): 170-1.

McLaughlin, Andrew C. *Report on the Diplomatic Archives of the Department of State, 1789-1840.* Washington: Carnegie Institution of Washington, 1904.

Millard, Thomas F. *America and the Far Eastern Question.* New York: Moffat, Yard, and Company, 1909.

Morris, Charles. *The War with Spain.* Philadelphia: J.B. Lippincott, 1899.

Nearing, Scott. *The American Empire.* New York: Rand School of Social Science, 1921.

"Our Public Land," *Far Eastern Review* 2, no. 3 (Aug. 1905), 58-9.

Paltsis, Victor Hugo. "Plan and Scope of a 'Manual of Archival Economy for the Use of American Archivists.'" *Annual Report of the American Historical Association* (1912): 253-64.

Parkhurst, Charles H. *The Philippine Islands: Their Permanent Tenure a Folly and a Crime: A Sermon Preached by Reverend Charles H. Parkhurst at the Madison Square Presbyterian Church, New York, November 24, 1898.* New York, 1898.

"The Philippine Situation," *Far Eastern Review* 5, no. 1 (Mar. 1909), 341-2.

"Proceedings of the First Annual Conference of Archivists, New York City, December 30, 1909." *Annual Report of the American Historical Association* (1909): 348.

Public Archives Commission. "Report of the Public Archives Commission." *Annual Report of the American Historical Association* (1900): 5-25.

———. "Report of the Public Archives Commission." *Annual Report of the American Historical Association* (1905): 329-40.

Quezon, Manuel. *Disposition of the Friar Lands.* Washington: Government Printing Office, 1912.

———. *The Jones Philippine Bill.* Washington: Government Printing Office, 1914.

"Recent Philippine Appointments and the Civil Service," *Far Eastern Review* 5, no. 12 (May 1909): 418.

Robert T. Swan. "Summary of the Present State of Legislation of the States and Territories Relative to the Custody and Supervision of the Public Records." *Annual Report of the American Historical Association* (1906): 13-21.

Robertson, James Alexander. "Notes on the Archives of the Philippines." *Annual Report of the American Historical Association* (1910): 421-26.

Rowland, Dunbar. "The Adaptation of Archives for Public Use." *Annual Report of the American Historical Association* (1912): 269-72.

———. "The Concentration of State and National Archives." *Annual Report of the American Historical Association* (1910): 293-98.

Schurman, Jacob Gould. *Philippine Affairs: A Retrospective and Outlook.* New York: Charles Scribner's Son's, 1902.

Swan, Robert. "Summary of the Present State of Legislation of the States and Territories relative to the Custody and Supervision of the Public Records." *Annual Report of the American Historical Association* Washington (1906): 15.

Taft, William Howard. *The Duty of Americans in the Philippines: Address by Hon. William Howard Taft, Civil Governor of the Philippines Islands, Delivered before the Union Reading College, Manila, P.I., Thursday, December 17, 1903.* Washington: Government Printing Office, 1904.

———. *The Philippines.* New York: Press of the Chamber of Commerce, 1904.

Taylor, Frederick. *The Principles of Scientific Management.* New York: W.W. Norton, 1911.

Taylor, John R.M., ed. *The Philippine Insurrection against the United States.* Pasay City, 1971.
Treaty of Paris. U.S.-Spain. Dec. 10, 1898. http://avalon.law.yale.edu/19th_century/sp1898.asp.
Turner, Frederick Jackson. *The Frontier in American History.* New York: Holt, Rinehart, and Winston, 1965.
United States. Treasury. *Letter from the Acting Secretary of the Treasury Transmitting Estimate of Appropriation for and Urging Necessity of the Construction of a National Archives Building, August 22, 1919.* Washington: Government Printing Office, 1919.
Van Laer, Arnold J.F. "Lessons of the Catastrophe in the New York States Capitol at Albany on March 29, 1911." *Annual Report of the American Historical Association* (1911): 331-36.
Virtue, Ethel B. "Principles of Classification for Archives." *Annual Report of the American Historical Association* (1914): 373-80.
Watterson, Henry. *History of the Spanish-American War.* New York: The Werner Company, 1898.
Williams, Daniel. *The Odyssey of the Philippine Commission.* Chicago: McClurg, 1913.
Willis, H. Parker. *Our Philippine Problem: A Study of American Colonial Policy.* New York: Henry Holt and Company, 1905.
Worcester, Dean. *Conditions in the Philippines: A Speech Delivered by Honorable Dean Conant Worcester at a Banquet in his Honor, Manila Hotel, October 13, 1913.* Manila: E.C. McCullough and Company, 1913.
Wright, Hamilton et al, *America Across the Seas: Our Colonial Empire.* New York: C.S. Hammond and Company, 1909.

Secondary Sources

Abinales, Patricio N. *Making Mindanao: Cotabato and Davao in the Formation of the Philippine Nation-State.* Quezon City: Ateneo de Manila University Press, 2000.
---. "Progressive-Machine Conflict in Early-Twentieth-Century U.S. Politics and Colonial State Building in the Philippines." In *The American Colonial State in the Philippines: Global Perspectives,* edited by Julian Go and Anne L. Foster, 148-181. Manila: Anvil, 2005.
Adas, Michael. "Improving on the Civilizing Mission? Assumptions of United States Exceptionalism in the Colonization of the Philippines." In *The New American*

Empire: A 21ˢᵗ Century Teach-In on U.S. Foreign Policy, edited by Lloyd C. Gardner and Marilyn B. Young, 153-181. New York: The New Press, 2005.

Agoncillo, Teodoro A. *History of the Filipino People*. Quezon City: Garotech Publishing, 1990.

Aguilar, Jr., Filomena V. *Clash of Spirits: The History of Power and Sugar Planter Hegemony on a Visayan Island*. Honolulu: University of Hawai'i Press, 1998.

Anderson, Warwick. *Colonial Pathologies: American Tropical Medicine, Race, and Hygiene in the Philippines*. Durham: Duke University Press, 2006.

---. "Where Every Prospect Pleases and Only Man Is Vile: Laboratory Medicine as Colonial Discourse." *Critical Inquiry* 18 (Spring 1992): 506-29.

Ando, Masashito. "From Destruction of Records to Recovery of Memory: Creating Archives in Asia." In *Creating an Archive Today*, edited by Toshie Awaya, 17-28. Tokyo: Tokyo University of Foreign Studies, 2005.

Appleman Williams, William. *Empire as a Way of Life: An Essay on the Cause and Character of America's Present Predicament Along with a Few Thoughts about an Alternative*. New York: Oxford University Press, 1980.

Battles, Matthew. *Library: An Unquiet History*. New York: Norton, 2003.

Bederman, Gail. *Manliness and Civilization: A Cultural History of Gender and Race in the United States, 1880-1917*. Chicago: University of Chicago Press, 1995.

Bennett, Tony. *The Birth of the Museum: History, Theory, Politics*. London: Routledge, 1995.

Birdsall, William Forest. "The American Archivists' Search for Professional Identity, 1909-1936." PhD diss., University of Wisconsin, 1973.

Bratlinger, Patrick. *Dark Vanishings: Discourse on the Extinction of Primitive Races, 1800-1930*. Ithaca, NY: Cornell University Press, 2003).

Briggs, Laura. *Reproducing Empire: Race, Sex, Science, and U.S. Imperialism in Puerto Rico*. Berkeley: University of California Press, 2002.

Brown, Dee. *Bury My Heart at Wounded Knee: An Indian History of the American West*. New York: Washington Square Press, 1981.

Cano, Gloria. "Blair and Robertson's *The Philippine Islands, 1493-1898*: Scholarship or Imperialist Propaganda?" *Philippine Studies* 56, no. 1 (2008): 3-46.

Cariño, Ledivina V. *A Dominated Bureaucracy: An Analysis of the Formulation of, and Reaction to, State Policies on the Philippine Civil Service*. Manila: College of Public Administration, University of the Philippines, 1989.

Césaire, Aimé. *Discourse on Colonialism*. Translated by Joan Pinkham. New York: Monthly Review Press, 2000.

Choy, Catherine Ceniza. *Empire of Care: Nursing and Migration in Filipino American History*. Durham: Duke University Press, 2003.

Clymer, Kenton J. *Protestant Missionaries in the Philippines, 1898-1916: An Inquiry into the American Colonial Mentality.* Urbana: University of Illinois Press, 1986.

Constantino, Renato. Introduction to *The Philippine Insurrection against the United States: A Compilation of Documents with Notes and Introduction,* edited by John R.M. Taylor, ix-xii. Pasig City: Eugenio Lopez Foundation, 1971.

–––. *The Miseducation of the Filipino.* Quezon City: Foundation for Nationalist Studies, 1982.

–––. *The Philippines: A Past Revisited.* Quezon City: Tala Publishing Services, 1975.

Cox, Richard. *American Archival Analysis: The Recent Development of the Archival Profession in the United States.* Metuchen, NJ: Scarecrow Press, 1990.

Cruz, Romeo V. *America's Colonial Desk and the Philippines, 1898-1934.* Quezon City: University o the Philippines, 1974.

Cullinane, Michael. *Ilustrado Politics: Filipino Elite Responses to American Rule, 1898-1908.* Quezon City: Ateneo de Manila University Press, 2003.

–––. "Implementing the 'New Order': The Structure and Supervision of Local Government During the Taft Era." In *Compadre Colonialism: Philippine-American Relations: 1898-1946,* edited by Norman G. Owen, 9-34. Manila: Solidaridad, [1971?].

Davies, D.W. *Public Libraries as Culture and Social Centers: The Origin and the Concept.* Metuchen, NJ: Scarecrow Press, 1974.

Delagoza, Fr. Rolando S. *History of the Philippine Civil Service.* Manila: Rex Printing Company, 1991.

Deloria, Jr., Vine. *Custer Died for Your Sins: An Indian Manifesto.* New York: Macmillan, 1969.

Doeppers, Daniel. *Manila, 1900-1941: Social Change in a Late Colonial Metropolis.* New Haven: Yale University Southeast Asian Studies, 1984.

Farrell, John T. "An Abandoned Approach to Philippine History: John R.M. Taylor and the Philippine Insurrection Records." *Catholic History Review* 39, no. 4 (1954): 385-407.

Findlay, Eileen J. Suárez. *Imposing Decency: The Politics of Sexuality and Race in Puerto Rico, 1870-1920.* Durham: Duke University Press, 1999.

Fry, Howard T. *A History of the Mountain Province.* Quezon City: New Day Publishers, 1983.

Gleek, Lewis. *American Institutions in the Philippines, 1898-1941.* Quezon City: R.F. Garcia, 1976.

Go, Julian. "Colonial Reception and Cultural Reproduction: Filipino Elites and United State Tutelary Rule." *Journal of Historical Sociology* 12, no. 4 (1999): 337-68.

Goldsby, Jacqueline. *A Spectacular Secret: Lynching in American Life and Literature.* Chicago: University of Chicago Press, 2006.

Gondos, Jr., Victor Gondos. *J. Franklin Jameson and the Birth of the National Archives, 1906-1926.* Philadelphia: University of Pennsylvania, 1981.

Gowing, Peter Gordon. *Mandate in Moroland: The American Government of Muslim Filipinos.* Diliman: University of the Philippines Press, 1977.

Graff, Henry F., ed. *American Imperialism and the Philippine Insurrection: Testimony Taken from Hearings on Affairs in the Philippine Islands before the Senate Committee on the Philippines, 1902.* Boston: Little, Brown, and Co., 1969.

Guererro, Milagros. "Luzon at War: Contradictions in Philippine Society, 1899-1902." PhD diss., University of Michigan, 1977.

de la Guzman, Abraham, ed. *Focus on the National Library: A Compilation of Papers Presented during an Orientation Seminar on the Policies and Functions of The National Library, September 7-10, 1964.* Manila: The National Library, 1964.

Halili, Jr., Servando D. *Iconography of the New Empire: Race and Gender Images and the American Colonization of the Philippines.* Quezon City: University of the Philippines Press, 2006.

Hernández, Vicente S. "Trends in Philippine Library History." *Libraries and Culture* 36, no. 2 (2001): 329-44.

Hoganson, Kristin L. *Fighting for American Manhood: How Gender Politics Provoked the Spanish-American and Philippine-American Wars.* New Haven, CT: Yale University Press, 1998.

Holt, Elizabeth Mary. *Colonizing Filipinas: Nineteenth-Century Representations of the Philippines in Western Historiography.* Quezon City: Ateneo de Manila University Press, 2002.

Ileto, Reynaldo. "Cholera and the Origins of the American Sanitary Order in the Philippines." In *Imperial Medicine and Indigenous Societies,* edited by David Arnold, 125-48. New York: Manchester University Press, 1988.

———. *Filipinos and their Revolution: Event, Discourse, and Historiography.* Quezon City: Ateneo de Manila University Press, 1998.

———. *Knowing America's Colony: A Hundred Years from the Philippine War.* Honolulu: University of Hawai'i Center for Philippines Studies, 1999.

———. *Pasyon and Revolution: Popular Movements in the Philippines, 1840-1910.* Quezon City: Ateneo de Manila University Press, 1979.

Jacobsen, Matthew Frye. *Barbarian Virtues: The United States Encounters Foreign Peoples at Home and Abroad, 1876-1917.* New York: Hill and Wang, 2000.

Jenista, Frank Lawrence. *The White Apos: American Governors on the Cordillera Central.* Quezon City: New Day Publishers, 1987.

Kalaw, Pura Villanueva. *How the Filipina Got the Vote.* Manila, 1952.

Kaplan, Amy. "Left Alone with America." In *Cultures of United States Imperialism*, edited by Amy Kaplan and Donald Pease, 3-21. Durham: Duke University Press, 1993.

Kaser, David. *A Book for Sixpence: The Circulating Library in America*. Pittsburgh: Beta Phi Mu, 1980.

Kerkvliet, Benedict. *The Huk Rebellion: A Study of Peasant Revolt in the Philippines*. Lanham, MD: Rowman and Littlefield, 2002.

Kinzer, Stephen. *Overthrow: America's Century of Regime Change from Hawaii to Iraq*. New York: Times Books, 2006.

Knuth, Rebecca. *Burning Books and Leveling Libraries: Extremist Violence and Cultural Destruction*. Westport, CT: Praeger, 2006.

---. *Libricide: The Regime-Sponsored Destruction of Books and Libraries in the Twentieth Century*. Westport, CT: Praeger, 2003.

Kramer, Paul. *The Blood of Government: Race, Empire, the United States and the Philippines*. Chapel Hill: University of North Carolina Press, 2006.

---. "The Water Cure." *New Yorker*, February 25, 2008. http://www.newyorker.com/reporting/2008/02/25/080225fa_fact_kramer.

Kwantes, Anne. *Presbyterian Missionaries in the Philippines: Conduits of Social Change, 1899-1910*. Quezon City: New Day Publishers, 1989.

LaFeber, Walter. *The New Empire: An Interpretation of American Expansion, 1860-1898*. Ithaca, NY: Cornell University Press, 1963.

Lindio-McGovern, Ligaya. *Filipino Peasant Women: Exploitation and Resistance*. Philadelphia: University of Pennsylvania Press, 1997.

Lott, Eric. *Love and Theft: Blackface Minstrelsy and the American Working Class*. New York: Oxford University Press, 1993.

Luton, Harry. "American Internal Revenue Policy in the Philippines to 1916." In *Compadre Colonialism: Philippine-American Relations: 1898-1946*, edited by Norman G. Owen, 65-80. Manila: Solidaridad, [1971?].

Mach, Thomas S. *"Gentleman George" Hunt Pendleton: Party Politics and Ideological Identity in Nineteenth-Century America*. Kent, OH: Kent State University Press, 2007.

Maranto, Robert and David A. Schultz. *A Short History of the United States Civil Service*. Lanham, MD: University Press of America, 1991,

May, Glenn Anthony. *Social Engineering in the Philippines: The Aims, Execution, and Impact of American Colonial Policy, 1900-1913*. Westport, CT: Greenwood Press, 1980.

McAlister, Melani. *Epic Encounters: Culture, Media, and U.S. Interests in the Middle East since 1945*. Berkeley: University of California Press, 2005.

McCoy, Alfred. "'An Anarchy of Families': The Historiography of State and Family in the Philippines." In *An Anarchy of Families: State and Family in the Philippines*, edited by Alfred McCoy, 1-30. Madison, WI: University of Wisconsin, Center for Southeast Asian Studies, 1993.

McKenna, Thomas M. *Muslim Rulers and Rebels: Everyday Politics and Armed Separatism in the Southern Philippines*. Berkeley: University of California Press, 1998.

Merry, Sally Engle. *Colonizing Hawai'i: The Cultural Power of Law*. Princeton: Princeton University Press, 2000.

Miller, Stuart Creighton. "The American Soldier and the Conquest of the Philippines." In *Reappraising an Empire: New Perspectives on Philippine-American History*, edited by Peter W. Stanley, 13-34. Cambridge: Harvard University Press, 1984.

---. *"Benevolent Assimilation": the American Conquest of the Philippines, 1899-1903*. New Haven: Yale University Press, 1982.

Mojares, Resil. *War Against the Americans: Resistance and Collaboration in Cebu, 1899-1906*. Quezon City: Ateneo de Manila University Press, 1999.

Morallos, Chando. *Treasures of The National Library: A Brief History of the Premier Library of the Philippines*. Manila: The National Library, 1998.

Morgan, Jennifer. *Laboring Women: Reproduction and Gender in New World Slavery*. Philadelphia: University of Pennsylvania Press, 2004.

National Archives. *Philippine National Archives: 100 Years, 1901-2001*. Manila: National Archives, 2001.

Nelson, William. *The Roots of American Bureaucracy*. Cambridge: Harvard University Press, 1982.

Ochosa, Orlino. *The Tinio Brigade: Anti-American Resistance in the Ilocos Provinces, 1899-1901*. Quezon City: New Day Publishers, 1989.

Omi, Michael and Howard Winant. *Racial Formation in the United States: From the 1960s to the 1980s*. New York: Routledge & Kegan Paul, 1986.

Osorio, Jonathan. *Dismembering Lāhui: A History of the Hawaiian Nation to 1887*. Honolulu: University of Hawai'i Press, 2002.

Owen, Norman G. "Introduction: Philippine Society and American Colonialism." In *Compadre Colonialism: Philippine-American Relations: 1898-1946*, edited by Norman G. Owen, 49-64. Manila: Solidaridad, [1971?].

Painter, Nell. *Standing at Armageddon: A Grassroots History of the Progressive Era*. New York: Norton, 2008.

Paredes, Ruby, ed. *Philippine Colonial Democracy*. New Haven, CT: Yale University Southeast Asia Studies, 1988.

Polestron, Lucien X. *Books on Fire: The Destruction of Libraries throughout History*. Translated by Jon E. Graham. Rochester, VT: Inner Traditions, 2007.

Rafael, Vicente. *White Love and Other Events in Filipino History*. Durham: Duke University Press, 2000.

Renda, Mary A. *Taking Haiti: Military Occupation and the Culture of U.S. Imperialism, 1915-1940*. Chapel Hill: University of North Carolina Press, 2001.

Reyes, Jose S. *Legislative History of American Economic Policy toward the Philippines*. New York: Columbia University, 1923.

Roces, Mina. "Is the Suffragist an American Colonial Construct? Defining 'the Filipino woman' in Colonial Philippines." In *Women's Suffrage in Asia: Gender, Nationalism, and Democracy*, edited by Louise Edwards and Mina Roces, 29. London: Routledge Curzon, 2004.

Roediger, David R. *The Wages of Whiteness: Race and the Making of the American Working Class*. London: Verso, 1991.

Rosenberg, Emily. *Spreading the American Dream: American Economic and Cultural Expansion, 1890-1945*. New York: Hill and Wang, 1982.

Ross, Rodney. "Waldo Gifford Leland: Archivist by Association." *American Archivist* 46, no. 3 (1983): 264-76.

Roth, Russell. *Muddy Glory: America's 'Indian Wars' in the Philippines, 1899-1935*. West Hanover, MA: The Christopher Publishing House, 1981.

Rozario, Kevin. *The Culture of Calamity: Disaster and the Making of Modern America*. Chicago: University of Chicago Press, 2007.

Rydell, Robert T. *All the World's a Fair: Visions of Empire at American International Expositions, 1876-1916*. Chicago: University of Chicago Press, 1984.

Said, Edward. *Orientalism*. New York: Vintage, 1979.

Salman, Michael. *The Embarrassment of Slavery: Controversies over Bondage and Nationalism in the American Colonial Philippines*. Berkeley: University of California Press, 2001.

Schirmer, Daniel. *Republic or Empire: American Resistance to the Philippine War*. Cambridge, MA: Schenkman Publishing, 1972.

Schultz, David and Robert Maranto. *The Politics of Civil Service Reform*. New York: Peter Lang Publishing, 1998.

Scott, William Henry. *Ilocano Responses to American Aggression, 1900-1901*. Quezon City: New Day Publishers, 1989.

Schellenberg, Theodore Roosevelt. *Modern Archives: Principles and Techniques*. Chicago: University of Chicago Press, 1956.

Shera, Jesse H. *Foundations of the Public Library: The Origins of the Public Library Movement in New England, 1629-1855*. Chicago: University of Chicago Press, 1949.

Silbey, David J. *A War of Frontier and Empire: The Philippine-American War, 1899-1902*. New York: Hill and Wang, 2006.

Silva, Noenoe. *Aloha Betrayed: Native Hawaiian Resistance to American Colonialism.* Durham: Duke University Press, 2005.
Simon, Louis. "Some Considerations on the Housing of Archives." *Annual Report of the American Historical Association* (1916).
Smith, Andrea. *Conquest: Sexual Violence and American Indian Genocide.* Boston: South End Press, 2005.
Sobritchea, Carolyn Israel. "American Colonial Education and Its Impact on the Status of Filipino Women." In *Women's Role in Philippine History: Selected Essays*, 79-108. Diliman: University of the Philippines Press, 1996.
Stannard, David. *Honor Killing: Race, Rape, and Clarence Darrow's Spectacular Last Case.* New York: Penguin Books, 2006.
Stoler, Ann. *Carnal Knowledge and Imperial Power: Race and the Intimate in Colonial Rule.* Berkeley: University of California Press, 2002.
Sullivan, Rodney. "Cholera and colonialism in the Philippines, 1899-1903." In *Disease, Medicine, and Empire*, edited by Roy MacLeod and Milton Lewis, 284-300. New York: Routledge, 1988.
---. *Exemplar of Americanism: The Philippine Career of Dean C. Worcester.* Ann Arbor: Center for South and Southeast Asian Studies, The University of Michigan, 1991.
Tinerella, Vincent P. "An Examination of John Franklin Jameson's Role as a Great Leader in the Establishment of the National Archives of the United States." *Illinois Libraries* 85, no. 3 (Spring 2005): 20-29.
de la Torre, Vistacion. *History of the Philippine Civil Service.* Quezon City: New Day Publishers, 1986.
Tucker, Louis Leonard. *Worthington Chauncey Ford: Scholar and Adventurer.* Boston: Northeastern University Press, 2001.
Veneracion, Jaime B. *Merit or Patronage: A History of the Philippine Civil Service.* Quezon City: Great Books Trading, 1988.
Vergara, Jr., Benito M. *Displaying Filipinos: Photography and Colonialism in Early 20th Century Philippines.* Quezon City: University of the Philippines Press, 1995.
Viola, Herman. *The National Archives of the United States.* New York: Harry N. Abrams, 1984.
Wells, Ida B., *Southern Horrors and Other Writings: The Anti-Lynching Campaign of Ida B. Wells, 1892-1900.* Edited by Jacqueline Jones Royster. Boston: Bedford/St. Martins, 1997.
Wermiel, Sara. *The Fireproof Building: Technology and Public Safety in the Nineteenth-Century American City.* Baltimore: The Johns Hopkins University Press, 2000.

Wexler, Laura. *Tender Violence: Domestic Visions in an Age of U.S. Imperialism.* Chapel Hill: University of North Carolina Press, 2000.

Wilgus, A. Curtis. "The Life of James Alexander Robertson." In *Hispanic American Essays: A Memorial to James Alexander Robertson,* edited by A. Curtis Wilgus, 3-9. Chapel Hill: The University of North Carolina Press, 1942.

Wills, Gary. *Lincoln at Gettysburg: The Words That Remade America.* New York: Simon and Schuster, 1993.

INDEX

Abinales, Patricio 8
Adams, Charles Francis
    work with Anti-Imperialist League 49-50, 52
    Civil War veteran experience 47-48
    investigation 55-56, 58
Aguinaldo, Emilio 34, 36, 38
American regime (see also United States regime)
    4, 12, 17, 19, 23, 77
American Historical Association 20, 23
Anderson, Warwick 6-8
anti-colonial perspectives 13
Anti-Imperialist League 13, 43, 47, 56, 73, 98
    creation of records/body of work 51-52, 59- 60, 92
    criticism of 45, 54
    role of 44, 49-50, 58
anti-imperialist movement 49- 51, 56, 59
    document creation 44- 45, 52, 60
anti-imperialist viewpoints 11, 46, 49, 50, 59, 92
archival history 1
archives and war 15-16, 18, 41, 45
    assessment of records 22
    necessity of records 28
Archives of Spain 18-19, 25-26
    (see also Spanish Archives)
Atkinson, Edward 49-50
    author of The Anti-Imperialist 52-54
    Vice-P resident of Anti-Imperialist League 52

Barrows, David
    A History of the Philippines 91
    former Philippine Commissioner 73, 75, 90
    public lands 75
    The Pacific Ocean in History 75
Benevolent Assimilation 3-4, 28, 86, 100, 102
Bell, J.F. 96
Blair, Emma Helen 20, 25, 59-60
Board on Geographical Names 84-85
    (see also Philippine Committee on Geographical Names)
Board of Surveys and Maps 85
British Museum 21
British occupation (of the Philippines) 21
Bureau of Archives 4, 5, 7, 9, 10-12, 14, 22, 24, 69-70, 74-75, 77, 79, 87, 93-94
    legacy/influence 100
    location (changes in) 70, 92, 99
    relationship to/with Bureau of Lands 75, 85
    responsibilities of Chief of the Bureau of Archives 69, 79
    role of/work of 77, 87, 98-100
    volume of records 98-99
Bureau of Archives, Patents Copyrights and Trademarks 70, 75, 83, 93
    (see also Bureau of Archives, Patents, Copyrights and Trademarks)
    work regarding cattle branding 82-83
Bureau of Forestry 75

Bureau of Insular Affairs (BIA) 8, 10, 79, 98
    chain of command 11, 25
    relationship with Philippine Library 25-26
    record creation/publication 31, 59
    role of 7, 26, 28, 30
    translation of records 33, 40
    volume of records 75, 98-99
Bureau of Labor 100
Bureau of Lands
(see also Bureau of Public Lands)
    Chief of the Bureau of Lands 67, 69
    core of colonial archive 85, 99
    establishment of 75, 84
    purpose of 70, 75, 85, 99
    Primer Containing Questions and Answers on the Public Land Laws in Force in the Philippine Islands 76-77
    public land inquiries/homesteading (see also public lands) 77-80
    working relationship with Bureau of Archives 7, 70, 74-75, 85, 87
Bureau of Mining 75
Bureau of Public Lands (see also Bureau of Lands)
    access to records 91, 94, 98
    An Act Creating a Bureau of Public Lands 17, 68, 100
    care for records 21
    role of Chief 69, 71
    classes of records 21, 27
    purpose of 67 r
    records generated by 68

carabao 81-82
    death of 81
    theft of 82-84
Carnegie, Andrew 2, 46-47, 49, 63
Carpenter, Frank W. 86
    Executive Secretary 73-74

Chief of Bureau of Insular Affairs 11
Civil Service Board 100
Civil War (United States) 43, 48-49
colonial archive 10, 12, 14, 85
    understanding of 13
    Spain-cession of 15, 39
    Spain-assessment of 22
    Spain-care for 26
    United States-development of 71, 85
colonial history 1
colonial rule
    archives 10, 95
    Philippines-independence from 15
    Spanish-in the Philippines 2
    United States -role of 8
    United States (in the Philippines) 1, 5, 7, 18, 24, 44, 50, 63, 65, 87, 97, 98-99
colonial state
    role of archives 5, 7, 9, 22, 92, 97, 100-101
    power of 7
    Spanish role 2, 5, 8, 9, 17, 21, 40, 72
    state of records 21, 67
    United States role 4, 6, 10, 61, 70, 85, 92, 100-101
    United States policies of 8
colonialism
    United States 4, 8, 10, 90, 92
    European 4, 8, 10
    Spanish 27
Constantino, Renato 30, 41
Court of Land Registration 68-69, 81
Crown lands 71
Cruz, Romeo V. 7, 8

Department of Education 94
Department of Fomento 39
Department of Justice 93
Department of the Interior 38, 67, 81

Department of Public Instruction (Philippines) 5, 93
Department of War (United States) 1, 13, 53
 (see also War Department)
  home of Bureau of Internal Affairs 28, 30, 40
Denby, Charles 54
Dewey, George 53-54
Edwards, Clarence Ransom 31-32
Elmer, Emma Osterman 95

Fergusson, A.W. 83, 99
Flag Law 13
Forbes, W. Cameron 32, 50
 arrival in Philippines 43
 Governor-General 43, 70-72, 74, 79, 86, 96
Ford, Worthington Chauncey
 administration of archives 24
 arguing for importance of Spanish archives 19, 20, 27-28
 background 20
 report on condition of archives 21-23

Gompers, Samuel 2, 7, 41

Harrison, Francis Burton
 administration 9, 10
 Governor-General 11, 89, 95-96
Harrison, (Benjamin) President 84
Hearst, William Randolph 3, 60
Hoar, George Frisbie 46-48, 50-51

Ide, Henry 59, 70
The Independent 55

Jingoist press 3
Jones Act 5, 50, 89, 93-95
Jones Bill 96

Jones, William A. 55-56
Jordan, David Starr 55

Kalaw, Maximo
 The Case for Filipinos (1916) 90, 91, 97
 critique of U.S. involvement with Philippines 91, 92, 94
 relationship to Teodoro Kalaw 95

Kalaw, Teodoro
 director of Philippine Library and Museum (1916) 9, 95, 97
 The Philippine Islands, 1493-1898 (Kalaw) 9, 11, 59, 89, 93

land allocation (see also Crown lands)
 controversy of 71-74, 86
 definition of types of land 74
 friar lands 64, 66
 leasing of public lands 80
 military reservations 64, 68
 private lands 64, 66
 public lands 10, 17, 64, 66, 69, 71, 73, 75, 76
  public land laws 73, 76
 purchase of 72-74
 purchase of public lands 77-78
 Spanish public land law 77
land patents 7
land records
 destruction of 65-66, 81
 generation of 78
 Spanish-land records 67, 77, 80
 United States-archive of land records 66, 68-70, 75-76, 80, 85-86
Land Registration Act (1902) 65, 68-69, 73-74, 84
 purpose of 76
 (see also Act 496 and Act 627) 68, 73

Land Registration Laws   86
    land registration (system of)   69
LeRoy, James   30-32, 51
Library of Congress   23, 29, 31
Lopez, Sixto   55, 58

MacArthur, Arthur (Military Governor)   64-65
Machine politicians   8
Marquardt, Walter William   95
May, Glen Anthony   8
McIntyre, Frank   72
    Chief of Bureau of Insular Affairs   26, 31, 59, 73
McKee, Syrena   95, 97
McKinley, William (U.S. President)
    "Benevolent Assimilation" policy   3, 4
    colonial rule   44
    response to anti-imperialists   53
    Schurman commission   54
Morris, Charles   49
Moses, Bernard   90, 91

Nearing, Scott   63, 65
notarial law   38

Official Gazette   68, 86
Office of Insurgent Records   30-32
Office of the Secretary of Agriculture, Industry and Commerce   36
Osmena, Sergio   51, 73
Otis, Elwell   54, 64
Owen, Norman G.   9

Painter, Nell Irvin   47
Parkhurst, Charles   45-47, 49
Philippine Assembly   89, 93
Philippine Autonomy Act (1916)   89
Philippine Commission   8, 18
    creation of Bureau of Public Lands   17
    development of Bureau of Archives   4, 16, 24, 67, 98
Philippine Committee on Geographical Names   85, 87
    (see also Board on Geographical Names)
Philippine Commission Report (1901)   19
    against anti-imperialism   57
    archival work   18, 25
    general legislation   27, 57-58, 65, 69, 75
    legacy   89
Philippine Division of Information   31
Philippine Government   36, 73, 86
    archives of   16, 26, 35
    census   36
    conflict with U.S.   64
    documents   28, 33, 41, 86
    jurisdiction   36, 73-74
    recordkeeping   34, 36
    relation to archives   33
    structure of   38, 39, 89, 97, 99
    works about   2
Philippine independence   15, 34, 50-51, 90, 92, 96
    declaration of   39
    opponents of   96
    supporters of   37, 55, 58, 73
Philippine Information Society   54
Philippine Legislature   71
Philippine Library   20, 95
    acquisition of material from Spain   25-27
Philippine Library and Museum   20
    creation of   5, 9, 93-94, 99-100
    evaluation of   95-97
Philippine Republic   54
    establishment of   36
    fighting American rule   15, 35

role of archives   30, 33, 38, 41, 98
Philippine Revolutionary Papers   16
(see also Philippine Insurgent Papers or Philippine Insurgent Records)
Philippine Insurgent Papers   16, 41
(see also Philippine Revolutionary Papers or Philippine Insurgent Records)
Philippine Insurgent Records   13, 16, 59
(see also Philippine Insurgent Papers)
Philippine investigation (see also Our Colonial Problem (Willis))   47, 55-56, 58
Philippine Revolution   10, 15, 29, 71
   genesis of   2
   role of   15
   suppression by U.S.   1
Philippine Revolutionary Government   13, 18
   importance of archives   30, 39
   management of records/archives   29, 39-40
   relations with U.S.   32
Philippine Senate   50, 89
Philippine-American War   39, 98
   context of   4, 6, 10, 15, 35, 43, 48, 64
   documents of/archives of   18, 29, 4
   official conclusion   49, 58, 60, 64, 92
   physical condition of records/archive   39, 74
   unofficial archive   44
presentism   101-102
Progressive politics   3
Progressive Era   8
Provisional Government of the Philippines   34
Public Lands Act (also Act 926)   74, 84
   (also Public Land Act)   69-71
   (also Act 926)   69
   (also Act 1128)   69
Public Land Law   76-79
   homesteads   78
   leasing   80
   purchase section   79

Quezon, Manuel   51-52
   American Occupation of the Philippines, 1898-1912   52
   Harrison's appointment to Governor General   95-96
   sale of friar lands   73
   Report of the Chief of the Bureau of Archives   19
   Republic or Empire? The Philippine Question   47

Rafael, Vicente   7
Reorganization Act (No. 1407)   93-94
Reorganization Act (No. 2572)   93
Reyes, Jose S.   66
Reynaldo Ileto   6, 68
Robertson, James Alexander   18-19, 28, 96-97
   First Director of Philippine Library (1910-1916)   9, 20, 25-27, 95
   "Notes on the Archive of the Philippines"   23-24
   report on state of Philippine archives   23-24
   The Philippine Islands, 1493-1898   20, 59-60
Roosevelt, Theodore (U.S. President)   11, 48, 58
Root, Elihu   58, 64
Rosario, M. del   37

Schurman, Jacob Gould
   anti-imperialist views   55
   chair of first Philippine Commission   54
   Philippine Affairs: A Retrospect and Outlook   55
Schurz, Carl   44, 46, 50, 52, 56
Sedition Law   13, 53, 58
Sleeper, Charles   72, 96

Spanish Archives   18, 22, 23, 25, 40, 75, 92
   (see also Spanish colonial archive)
   cession of   16, 19, 26, 39-40, 92
   importance of   18, 75
Spanish colonial archives (see also Spanish Archives)   19, 22- 23, 25, 33-34
   assessment of   22
Spanish colonial government   38, 67
   records of   40, 74, 80
   legislation   77
Spanish colonial rule   2
Spanish Government
   archives under   9, 19, 38, 99
   destruction of records   18-19
   transfer of colonial records   25, 27, 74
Spanish records   17, 32
   body of records   85, 99
   cession of (Spanish archives)   61, 67
Spanish regime (see also Spanish government)   4
   creation of archives   12, 32, 74, 76-77
   care of archives   21, 98
   improvement upon   10
   importance of archives   20
   public works   65
   transfer of colonial records   17, 19
Spanish-American War   3, 10
   archives as trophies   18, 28
   end of   16, 19, 27-28, 35, 41
   historical importance   15, 49, 91-92
   state of public records   21, 16, 18, 27-28, 35
   state of records/assessment   20, 23
Spanish land records   65-67, 77, 80
Spanish land laws   77
Stoler, Ann Laura   13
Storey, Moorfield
   President of Anti-Imperialist League   43, 50-51President of the NAACP   43

Taft Commission   11
   (see also United States Philippine Commission (second))
Taft era (1900-1913)   8, 9, 11
   end of   89, 93
Taft, William Howard   1
   as U.S. President   47, 73
   campaign for President   30
   effect on colonial policy   10, 77, 96
   Governor-General   52, 64, 72, 86
   response to anti-imperialists   45, 55, 58
   roles in government   11, 44
Tavera, Pardo de   84, 91
Taylor, John R. M.   16, 28-29, 60
   commonplace book   29
   Compilation of Philippine Insurgent Records   29-30, 33, 35, 40-41, 59
   publishing controversy   31-33
Thomas, Nicholas   7
Tinio, Manuel   96
Treasury Department-Philippines   38
Treaty of Paris   2
   acquisition of archives for U.S.   15-19, 22, 25, 28, 39, 41, 71, 74
   ceding of public lands   64, 66
   interpretation   28
   ratification of   3, 6
   value of archives   27
Turner, Frederick Jackson   2, 63
United States colonial administration   13, 23, 25, 77
United states colonial government   5, 12, 33, 43, 65, 81, 84-85
United states colonial government archives   22, 33
   importance of   100-101
United States colonial rule   1, 18, 24, 65, 87, 97-98

United States colonial state   8, 61
United States Department of War   13, 28
United States Geographic Board   85
United States Philippine Commission (first)   54
   (see also Schurman Commission)
   legislation regarding land laws   64, 66,72, 75
   legislation regarding cattle   82

United States Philippine Commission (second)
   1, 11, 55 (see also Taft Commission)
United States-Philippine relations   3-5, 7, 48, 61
United States regime (see also American regime)
   28, 71

U.S.S. Maine   2-3

War Department (U.S.)   33
Warren, Fiske   50, 58
Watterson, Henry   15
Wells, Ida B.   46
Welsh, (Herbert)   56
Willis, H. Parker   51
   investigation of Philippine conditions   52, 56-58
   Our Colonial Problem   58
   Our Philippine Problem: A Study of American Colonial Policy (1905)   57-58
Wilson, Woodrow (U.S. President)   11, 89, 96
Winslow, Erving   49, 50-52,71
   Executive Bureau   5, 93-94
Worcester, Dean   90-91, 96
   friar land controversy   73-74, 86
   member of Schurman Commission   54
   Secretary of the Interior   31, 51, 90
   support of colonial policy   90
Wright, Luke E.   32, 68-69

yellow journalism   15, 59

Yriarte, Manuel   91
   Chief of the Division of Archives-Spain   25-26
   consolidation of records   19
   Chief of the Bureau of Archives-Spain   9, 17, 19, 24, 26, 28, 94

Zulueta, Clemente J.   25

www.ingramcontent.com/pod-product-compliance
Lightning Source LLC
Chambersburg PA
CBHW021357300426
44114CB00012B/1266